CHARDONNAY

By the same author:
Making Sense of Wine Tasting
An Encounter with Wine
Australian Wines and Wineries
Australia–New Zealand Wine Year Book
The Wolf Blass Story

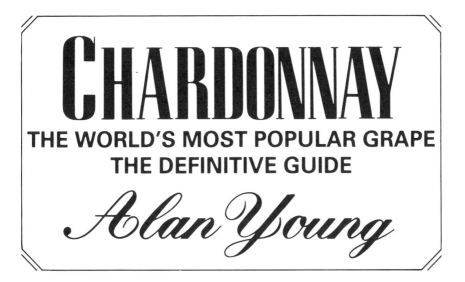

CHARDONNAY

THE WORLD'S MOST POPULAR GRAPE
THE DEFINITIVE GUIDE

Alan Young

Foreword by Christian Pol Roger

SIDGWICK & JACKSON
LONDON

First published in Great Britain in 1988
by Sidgwick & Jackson Limited

ISBN 0-283-99604-8

All maps drawn by Neil Hyslop

Phototypeset by Rowland Phototypesetting Limited
Bury St Edmunds, Suffolk
Printed by Butler & Tanner Limited, Frome and London
for Sidgwick & Jackson Limited
1 Tavistock Chambers, Bloomsbury Way
London WC1A 2SG

For Robert Mondavi

CONTENTS

Part Three: Chardonnay in the Vineyard

Part Four: Making Chardonnay

ACKNOWLEDGEMENTS

An endless list of people, companies and institutions around the world contributed to this work. I hope that they realize the part they played and the amount of gratitude I owe them for their support. Due to the global nature of the work, these people are everywhere from the South Island of New Zealand to the far-flung corners of Canada and Europe.

In the UK enormous support came from the 'boys and girls' of Ostler's, Robert Joseph and the staff of *Wine* magazine, Helen Verdcourt, and Peter and Penny Duff.

Thanks are due to the wine companies of Champagne, notably Pol Roger, Deutz, Dom Ruinart, Henriot, Taittinger and Mumm, who all contributed to the Champagne studies in Australia, France and the USA. And particular thanks to Arnaud de Mareuil and his PR staff at Moët & Chandon and Château Saran. The CIVC and its officers were gracious in their support.

Raymond Bernard of ONIVIN, Dijon, Robert Drouhin, Jean-Charles Servant of FIB, Beaune, Bernard Jaillet and W. D. Hardy all helped check the facts about Burgundy. A special thanks to Pierre Poupon for allowing the re-print of statistics from his classic work, *Atlas des Grands Vignobles de Bourgogne.*

From many Californians, the help was generous; in particular, Don Neel, Richard Arrowood, Paul Dolan, Jed Steele, Bob Mueller, Zelma Long, Dr Richard Petersen, Philip Hiaring, Larry Walker and Tucker Catlin.

Much of the important research work was not in English. The translation skills of Helen Verdcourt, Heather Moody, Elaine Barry and Bill Hardy are gratefully acknowledged. I am especially grateful to Serena Sutcliffe, MW, and Helen Verdcourt for granting me the wealth of their specialist knowledge when it came to the Burgundy chapter. Both ladies have dealt with the broad spectrum of Burgundy producers over the years and also conduct education programmes about the area. Richard Cirami, Drs Brian Freeman and Andrew Markides, Brenton Baker and Murray Stannard contributed to the viticulture chapter. Much of the soils chapter was adapted from the CSIRO book *Soils*; the balance was from my book *Australian Wines and Wineries*. Dr Paul Monk, Clayton Cone, Alan Hoey and Monsieur Billion helped breathe technical excellence into the winemaking chapter. The staff and officers of the Australian Wine Research Institute, and the Society of Viticulture and Oenology kindly gave permission to quote from their publications and provided considerable personal support.

A very unexpected source of assistance came from the staff members of the Vineland and Summerland research stations in Canada. Particularly, I thank Dr Helen Fisher and John Barkovic for their help in exposing the full facts about winegrowing in their country.

Four very special people gave their all to make this manuscript readable: Helen Martin-Beck, who has typed each of my seven books, Nancy Whittle and Peter Saunders who pre-edited the work before it finally ended in Carey Smith's lap at Sidgwick & Jackson. And last, but by no means least, my friend Larry King for the support and kindness he extended to make this work possible. To each of them, at least a million thanks.

LIST OF MAPS

WEIGHTS AND MEASURES RELATING TO WINEGROWING

We are still a divided world, especially when it comes to weights and measures. We have the metric system, the imperial system and the American system which is neither or both, but employs bits of each of the other two and a few local titbits.

For the sake of simplicity, this book has mainly used the metric system, with the exception of the USA chapters where the local parlance is used. For residents of countries that do not, or will not, use the international system of measurement, here are some conversions.

One hectare = 2.47 acres (roughly 2½ acres)
One litre = 100 centilitres (cl) = 1.05 US quarts or 33.8 fluid ounces.
One hectolitre (hl) = 100 litres = 22 imperial or 26.42 US gallons.
One hectolitre also = 11 cases of 12 × 750 ml bottles
40 hectolitres/hectare = 3 tonnes per acre, roughly
One Burgundy barrel (*une pièce*) = 220–228 litres of wine, or about 25 cases of wine (barrels in Chablis, Bordeaux and some other regions hold varying amounts)

To convert:

Millimetres to inches	divide by 25.4
Kilometres to miles	multiply by 0.621
Miles to kilometres	multiply by 1.609
Acres to hectares	multiply by 0.405
Kilograms to pounds	multiply by 2.205
Pounds to kilograms	divide by 2.25

(One tonne of grapes is about 60 cases of wine)

Litres to gallons imperial	divide by 4.54
Litres to gallons US	divide by 3.78
Fahrenheit to centigrade	subtract 32° × ⁵⁄₉
Centigrade to fahrenheit	multiply by ⁹⁄₅ + 32°

US dollars are used throughout the book

FOREWORD
by Christian Pol Roger

I am happy to write a few lines of introduction to Alan Young's excellent book on Chardonnay – the grape variety which plays such a fundamental role in the production of Champagne (which is particularly appropriate in this case, since Alan is known to his closest friends as 'Champagne Al').

My personal enthusiasm for a book on such a complex grape variety goes without question. Such a study is of significant interest to all of us who have at heart the understanding and appreciation of the present and future role of the Chardonnay grape.

This very fine publication is something of a reflection of the man himself. While it reflects his great knowledge of the specific grape variety, it is also, in the larger sense, a mirror of his mind and his great sincerity. He shows us how Chardonnay, 'born' in the Mediterranean region, has won approval and taken a significant place in the international world of wine. Equally valuable is the fact that he has focused on another important issue which has long concerned him: that universality of knowledge is not necessarily the same thing as universality of taste. The enormous variety of soils and regions, the specific nature of climatic pockets and the astounding diversity of people's concepts and expectations mean that the noble grape variety is to the world of viticulture what the individual mind is to the human race.

The soundness of the technical research that has been carried out on the grape, and the wines that it produces, opens up vast horizons of subtleties and nuances of taste, as well as judgements and feelings of the tasters. It is this aspect of the book which will be particularly valuable for the reader who sees the act of tasting as above all an act of humility.

For my part, I want to thank Alan Young for having, with this masterly work, contributed to our understanding of the history of wine, and in particular to that of Chardonnay, often considered by those in the profession to be the queen of the white varieties.

AUTHOR'S PREFACE

Every wine-producing country has its share of great men and women working in the fields of wine research, viticulture, oenology and marketing. But for the past two decades one man, Robert Mondavi, has dominated the centre stage. He has been a tireless innovator: in every facet of wine, excellence is the only standard he knows.

The pages of this book will point out that comparative judgements of wine, particularly those of Chardonnay, are of little real use. Despite this, and regardless of whether the tastings are held in Hong Kong, London, Perth or France, the Robert Mondavi Chardonnay is always among the most popular wines. The justifiably famous Puligny-Montrachet winemaker, Vincent Leflaive, following a tasting in the heart of white Burgundy country, paid Bob the ultimate left-handed compliment, 'Il peut faire un sacré vin, cet animal Mondavi!' ('He can make one hell of a wine, that guy Mondavi!')

This book, about the world's most popular white wine grape, could only be dedicated to the man who has pioneered the way in the New World and, at the same time been so instrumental in improving standards in the Old. The marvellous thing about the Mondavi dynasty is that there are a lot more Mondavis to come – if Bob ever calls it a day.

Please raise your favourite glass of Chardonnay and drink a toast to Robert Mondavi, a man of great humility and the winemaker of the century.

INTRODUCTION
Chardonnay:
The Elusive Definition

There must be a thousand books about Bordeaux, hundreds covering Burgundy, and a like number on the subject of grapes generally. Yet, even though Chardonnay is by far the world's most preferred varietal wine style (more than 600 wineries in the USA alone make at least one Chardonnay), there is not, to my knowledge, a single book that covers the wine consumers' favourite tipple.

This does not mean that nothing is written about Chardonnay. On the contrary, there is too much, far too much, nonsense written about this phenomenon. When it is said that a wine has 'typical' Cabernet, Riesling, Gewürztraminer or almost any other wine flavour, most people have some idea of what is meant. With Chardonnay it is a very different story. Not only is there no such thing as typical Chardonnay, there is also no typical California, New York, Barossa or New Zealand Chardonnay. Anybody who thinks there is should go straight back to the drawing board. The styles of Chablis, Meursault, and Mâcon are as clearly signposted as the roads to those villages. Not so with varietal Chardonnays from the New World. If proof was ever needed, a set of international evaluations conducted in France, England, the USA and Australia proved this point conclusively. As an essential part of this book, I decided to examine the question of cultural differences as a factor in evaluating the same stimuli – in this case a range of Chardonnays from around the world. Fasten your seat belts for the results!

One event was conducted in Beaune, France, the other in London, England, with the co-operation of *Wine* magazine. The Burgundy panel consisted of fourteen winemakers, the London one of six Masters of Wine, seven press and trade representatives and myself. The judges tasted twenty-seven wines in all (five from Australia, one from Bulgaria, one from Chile, eleven from France, two from Italy, one from New Zealand, one from Spain and five from California). The wines are listed below in order of tasting, along with the top dozen wines, in alphabetical order, in each country.

What appeared at first to be a simple exercise, actually turned out to be an unconscious battle between Old and New World philosophies. It was abundantly clear that tasters in the two countries do not judge wines in the same way. Surprisingly, the Beaune panel

RESULTS OF CHARDONNAY EVALUATIONS
(in alphabetical order)

LONDON, UK

1983	Acacia	Carneros, CA	USA
1985	Cooks	Hawkes Bay	New Zealand
1984	Jean Leon	Penedès	Spain
1982	Leeuwin Estate	Margaret River, WA	Australia
1983	Robert Mondavi	Napa Valley	USA
1983	Petaluma	South Australia	Australia
1983	Leflaive Clavoillon	Puligny-Montrachet	France
1985	Rosemount Estate	Denman, NSW	Australia
1983	Simi	Sonoma Valley, CA	USA
1985	Tyrrells	Pokolbin, NSW	Australia
1984	Wagner	Finger Lakes, NY	USA
1985	Z.D.	California	USA

BEAUNE, FRANCE

1983	Acacia	Carneros, CA	USA
1985	Joseph Drouhin	Bourgogne Blanc	France
1985	Cooks	Hawkes Bay	New Zealand
1982	Leeuwin Estate	Margaret River, WA	Australia
1984	Antonin Rodet	Mercurey, Ch de Cham	France
1982	Lafon	Meursault Charmes	France
1983	Robert Mondavi	Napa Valley, CA	USA
1983	Petaluma	South Australia	Australia
1985	Leger-Plumet	Pouilly-Fuisse	France
1984	Carillon	Puligny-Montrachet	France
1983	Leflaive Clavoillon	Puligny-Montrachet	France
1983	Frescobaldi	Pomino	Italy

considered twenty-seven wines 'too many' to evaluate seriously at one go.

The results showed an enormous gulf in the perception of fundamental measurable, objective criteria such as acid, oak, fruit and sulphur. Oak was the main point of disagreement, particularly with the Australian and New York wines. A majority of UK judges marked these wines as having dominant oak, yet this went almost unnoticed by the Burgundian panel.

In many cases, the two panels made absolutely contradictory remarks about the same wines. A wine from Wagner Vineyards in New York was judged as one of the six best in London, but drew seven 'not good' comments from the Beaune panel, who placed it in their *bottom* six. In fact, the London judges praised the very characteristics that most upset the French. Conversely, the London panel did not find the complexity that appealed to the French judges in either the Drouhin Bourgogne Blanc or the Rodet Château de Chamirey.

These judgements also showed that wine tasters in each country have their own philosophy about what constitutes Chardonnay, let alone a 'good' Chardonnay. With rare exceptions, Burgundian winemakers are quick to spot a 'foreigner' and, irrespective of how well a particular wine is regarded in its own or any other country, in Burgundy it will more than likely be dismissed as 'short, flat and without interest', 'not Chardonnay', or more simply described as 'a joke'.

Maybe this is attributable to the basic Burgundian philosophy that a Chardonnay that tastes like a varietal wine is coarse and vulgar. A white Burgundy, it is argued, should taste like the vineyard or town of its origin – what the French call *'le goût de terroir'*. This is what separates a Meursault from a Mâcon, or a Chablis from a Côte Chalonnaise.

Conversely, when expensive white Burgundies are evaluated in the New World, one is likely to hear such comments as 'lacking in fruit', 'green', 'too yeasty', 'simple', 'dirty' or 'musty'.

When I take a highly regarded Australian Chardonnay to New Zealand, invariably the first question is, 'What variety is this?' Strangely, this does not happen when a similar wine is tasted in California or New York, which possibly means that American and Australian Chardonnays have a degree of similarity. Does all this merely confirm the belief of Burgundian winemaker, Robert Drouhin – that only Burgundians can and should judge Burgundy wines, and only Californians should judge California wines? And does this not call into question the validity of cross-cultural judgements – whether they be of films, music, theatre or wine? Maybe not, but it does bear out one point: there may be a definitive Chablis or Mâcon, but there is no such thing as a definitive Chardonnay.

Maybe the point is better illustrated by a breakfast meeting I had at the Yountville Diner in California. Over coffee and cereal, I asked Robert Mondavi, 'What is the flavour of Chardonnay?' He looked at me rather quizzically and said three simple words, 'I don't know!' Turning to his eldest son, Michael, who is president of the Robert Mondavi winery, he put the same question, and was given the same reply. Now, if arguably the *best* exponent of the variety finds it impossible to define the flavour, what hope is there for the rest of us?

The aim of this book is to unravel such complexities, to explain the contributions of different clones and climates, the myths about soil and sites, and to explore the origins of the myriad nuances of flavour found in Chardonnay, from Chablis to Chile. If it were not for this wide range of flavours, one doubts that the Chardonnay craze would have been so international. The very fact that a Mâcon Chardonnay tastes different – and has a different price tag from wine produced in Marlborough, New Zealand – is the very charm of the variety. Had Chardonnay been a stay-at-home variety like Pinot Noir, its Burgundian red blood-brother, most of us would never have tasted the wine.

The excitement aroused by developments in California opened the door for Australia, then New Zealand, Spain, Italy, Central Europe and South America, to display their talents with the grape. And each success has brought new flavours, lower prices and a quickening of interest in the wine style.

The graphs on pages 8 and 9 illustrate the origins of the wine's flavours and should go a long way towards explaining the wonderful choices open to the wine lover, while on the other hand showing why there is no such thing as a 'typical' Chardonnay flavour – unless one thinks that limes taste like peaches, or apricots like butter. Flavour is paramount to me. Frankly, I care far less about who made the wine, where it comes from, which way the slope faces, or who planted the last vine, than I do about how a wine actually *tastes*.

In the course of my research, many hundreds of wonderful (and terrible) bottles were opened and evaluated in the company of the most respected authorities on each aspect of providing flavour – whether it be French oak, Canadian yeast, California clones, New Zealand rootstocks or Australian pruning. But it is *you* who are the ultimate judge. What you like is the world's best wine – and no one can contest that – but I hope that these pages will open up new experiences and areas of understanding for you.

Happy reading!

Alan Young
London 1988

PART ONE

The Origins of Chardonnay

The History

'When we hold up a glass of wine, what is in it? There is relaxation, there is reward, there is reflection, there is the key to communion, a link with the past and a very great touch with the earth. If these things aren't associated with good health, I don't know what is.'

Alex Cohen,
Perth Physician

Vines are indigenous to all continents except Australasia. There are many classifications of grape vines, but the ones that concern us most are the Eurasian *Vitis vinifera* and the native-American *Vitis labrusca*.

Evidence clearly suggests that *vinifera* wines came from an area to the south of the Caspian and Black Seas, and have thrived since time immemorial in warm climates – that part of the globe between 30–50° north and 30–42° south of the Equator. *Vitis vinifera*, the family to which Chardonnay belongs, tends to perform best when grown in regions that provide long, warm-hot, dry summers, and cool winters.

That, at any rate, is its historical preference. However, modern know-how has taken the vine, and Chardonnay in particular, to climates where fifty years ago it was impossible to grow viable crops. This has been brought about by more careful selection of vineyard locations, the development of rootstocks, improved clones and ever-evolving viticultural techniques.

Where Chardonnay originally came from is anybody's guess, and I mean guess. Enquiries among leading scholars of the classics, botany, history and viticulture have unearthed three possible origins. A strong body of opinion suggests it must have come from a warm-hot area due to its inherent ability to perform well in these types of areas – one of the rare few 'noble' varieties that does. The aspirants in this case are Caucasia and Syria/Lebanon, a proposal that not surprisingly, has tremendous support in those places!

Not often do I meet a man with the firm conviction of Claude Taittinger of Champagne fame. He is adamant that Chardonnay's birthplace is Cyprus, a proposal that enjoys very little, if any, support.

As one authority puts it, 'The whole question of research into this area of history and winemaking is fraught with the problem of finding original source material that has not been "adapted" or misquoted by subsequent authors; it is too painfully easy to be selective in support of the argument you wish to prove, in defiance or deliberate ignorance of other equally valid material.'

What could be considered as authoritative French works of the last century suggest that Chardonnay is native to Burgundy, for example. Needless to say, this theory is popular among the French, but it is difficult to validate.

In many countries, the correct meaning of grape varieties is a continuing source of confusion. In the USA, Riesling is called Johannisberg Riesling, Australians (the kings of misnomers) refer to Syrah as either Shiraz or Hermitage but never by its correct name, and in France Chardonnay has so many synonyms that it is hard to know what's what. That does not matter that much, though, as a wine in France is almost never called by its varietal name; everything is generically Champagne, Chablis, Jura, Mâcon or whatever.

For the outsider it is not that easy, as it is only in the last two decades that it has been proved that Chardonnay is *not* a member of the Pinot family, even though a gathering of French scientists in Lyon as long ago as 1872 determined that Chardonnay was a separate and non-Pinot variety. In Chablis, the variety is known as Beaunois, Aubaine in Chassagne and Puligny-Montrachet, Melon d'Arbois in the Jura and Epinette Blanche in Champagne. The Germans know it as Weisser Clevner, and various groups around the globe have called or do call it Pinot Blanc Chardonnay, Chardennet, Pinot Blanc à Cramant, Rousseau, Mâconnais, Gamay Blanc, Petite Sainte-Marie or ever Gelber Weissburgunder. In Lebanon it is known as Meroue or Obakeh. No one else can have an identity problem to compare with that of Chardonnay. We have nowhere near completed the list of names, and, in addition, there is a Chardonnay Musque (Muscat) with strong Muscaty flavours, as well as a cross-bred variety.

There can be little wonder that, as a varietal, it did not take off earlier in the New World. That happened soon after 1974 when it became officially recognized in France and California as Chardonnay – and nothing else – parallel with the development of superior clones.

Scientists identify grapevines by the cane, growing tips, leaf, shoot and cluster. Even though the leaf shape is very similar, Chardonnay differs from the Pinot family in a number of ways. It is more vigorous and the leaves are smoother and roll back at the edge rather than fold in about the mid-rib. Chardonnay is also free of hair on the leaf's lower surface. The bunches are larger than Pinot, not quite as compact and the berries are round rather than slightly oval. Obviously there are more technical details about the leaf shape, that being beyond the scope of this work, but in a word or three, the naked base of the Petiolar sinus, as in Chardonnay, is not found in any Pinot.

Characteristics

Chardonnay could be classified as the 'sweetheart' of the grapegrower, the winemaker and the consumer. For the grapegrower its most appealing feature is a short growing season, allowing it to be grown in regions such as Champagne and Burgundy where there are a limited number of summer days. As an example, the Champagne laws dictate that the fruit (Chardonnay and both Pinots) will be harvested 100 days after flowering, whereas for Cabernet Sauvignon, in the Napa Valley this time is more like 130 days.

In one area of Australia where the seasons are six months ahead of the northern hemisphere, Chardonnay will have budburst on or about 7 September, flowering about 1–7 November, and will be harvested in mid-February, whereas Cabernet Sauvignon, with budburst and flowering at much the same time as Chardonnay, will not be harvested at the end of March or even in April. This 40–60 days' longer growing period would make it impossible for Cabernet to be grown in regions with short summers; the fruit would never ripen.

On this minus side, the early budburst poses a problem in regions such as Chablis, Champagne, Burgundy, upstate New York, and other areas with long winters. The delicate little buds can be burnt off by late frosts, killing the crop before the season even

starts. Other than this one problem, Chardonnay crops gener-
ously, is relatively disease free, commands top prices and is often
described as the most 'forgiving' variety.

Yet, strangely, unlike most other wine grapes, when picked
fresh in the vineyard it has very little varietal flavour unless very
ripe. Its ability to yield good quality fruit under the widest range
of viticultural conditions, is what makes it so ideal. California
growers are normally delighted with the yields of Chardonnay; I
will never forget the look on a French winemaker's face when he
was told about yields of twenty tonnes per hectare in an Australian
irrigated region.

As a rule, winemakers love Chardonnay. Here is a wine that can
have simple fruit flavours when made without oak barrel ageing
yet enormous complexity when carefully moulded by a craftsman.
While it has been said that it is difficult to make poor wine from
Chardonnay, at least 50 per cent of the wines I taste are poor to
shocking. For some reason, novices in the handling of Chardonnay
think it has to be swamped with new oak flavour. This became very
obvious in my international evaluations, the tyro winemakers
being easily detected by the amount of oak in a mixture that I would
only jokingly refer to as wine.

Generic or Varietal?
As we have seen, the most important factor that came out of these
international judgings was that people from different countries
have different criteria for assessing quality. For me, these tastings
showed that white Burgundy or Chablis or Mâcon are definitely
generic wines. Even though made from 100 per cent Chardonnay,
none of these wines is meant to taste like a varietal Chardonnay as
known in the New World. White Burgundy and Chardonnay are
apples and oranges, not apples and apples.

Vineyard Personality
'Varietal orientation' is largely a New World invention. Most of us
have discovered wine as adults, and have done so rapidly and
avidly. Inevitably, we have sought tools to hasten the learning
process. I feel that varietal character has served this purpose, but is
now accorded over-riding importance. In France, it remains a
secondary factor in winemaking and winetasting.

The French feel that the noble varieties owe their rank to evolved
or elaborated flavours, and that Cabernet Sauvignon or Pinot Noir
character *in itself* is not noble. A Chardonnay that tastes like
Chardonnay is considered a coarse, vulgar wine. A decent red

Burgundy may taste like Pinot Noir, but a fine red Burgundy tastes like its place, or better yet, its vineyard of origin. This notion is seldom discussed specifically, but it comes up obliquely in discussions between Burgundy growers: that shipper makes good wines, but none of them tastes like the village named on the label. Local character is, indeed, at the heart of French viticultural thinking.

These ideas have been backed up by Thierry Matrot of Meursault's top-priced Domaine Joseph Matrot. Speaking at what was probably the world's first international Chardonnay seminar, 'Focus on Chardonnay' – a Sonoma Valley event that attracted the heavyweights of France and California – he said, 'As a Burgundian, I want to preserve the personality of each vineyard.' Several of the French contingent at the seminar echoed this sentiment. At the same event Zelma Long of the Simi Winery, stated that the Californian approach is entirely the opposite. In the first place they determined what style of wine they wanted to make and then contracted growers to supply grapes that filled these requirements.

To achieve a 'vineyard personality' in the finished bottle of wine, one might suggest that it was necessary for the grapes to come from a single vineyard. In fact, this is a rather rare situation in Burgundy where the vineyards are relatively small by most standards. In fact, less than 50 per cent is bottled in such a manner, and this is is done mainly by the high-profile producers – the wines you hear and read about in the wine columns but rarely, if ever, get to drink. Even these people sell a portion of their wine, in some cases a large portion, to the *négociants* who blend wines of numerous vineyards, and even districts, to make the well-known labels seen in wine stores around the world.

The following figures from Meursault and Puligny Montrachet (quoted in Anthony Hanson's book *Burgundy*), give some idea of vineyard holdings and of the percentage of production bottled at the winery; the balance is sold as unfinished wine:

Heritiers Darnat: 1 hectare, 30 per cent bottled at the estate
Domaine Charles Giraud: 9 hectares, 30 per cent bottled at the estate
Domaine des Comtes Lafon: 12 hectares, 75 per cent bottled at the estate
Charles Alexant: 5 hectares, 100 per cent bottled at the estate
Domaine Joseph Matrot: 15 hectares, 65 per cent bottled at the estate
Domaine Carillon Père et Fils: 10 hectares, 30 per cent bottled at the estate

Domaine Leflaive: 18 hectares, 65 per cent bottled at the estate
Domaine Etienne Sauzet: 12 hectares, 80 per cent bottled at the
  estate

With the ebb and flow of vintage variations, caused by capricious weather, there is no such thing as 'average' annual production. However, it is possible to obtain some sort of figure for each decade, which will throw a little light on yields per hectare.

From 1950 to 1960 yields were about 30 hectolitres (hl) per hectare. This was, possibly, the period when Burgundy's Chardonnay vineyards reached their all-time low, not necessarily in yields but in vine health. The introduction of clonally selected vines over the following decades saw yields increase to 37 hl per hectare by 1970 and 70 hl per hectare by 1980, or an increase from 407 dozen bottles/hectare to a possible 770 dozen/hectare. At an average price of $250 per dozen one doesn't need to be a mastermind to realize the importance of this work, and the financial return for the Burgundian grower. Little wonder that some people can exist on one single hectare when prices are up around $600 per case!

Chardonnay makers in California, Australia and other New World countries may have vineyards at least four times the size of these French holdings, and may bottle all of their wines themselves, but even though their yields may be somewhat more generous and reliable than Burgundy, they are not able to command the same prices; yet.

CHARDONNAY DESCRIPTORS DERIVED FROM:

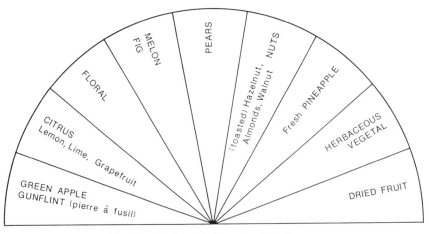

Fig. 1   Cool/cold climate viticulture

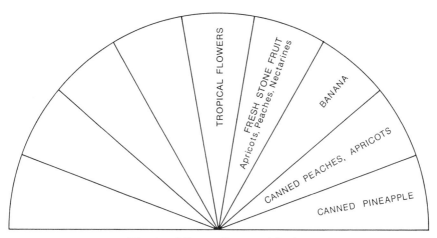

Fig. 1a Warm climate viticulture

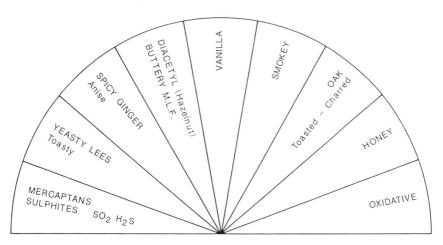

Fig. 1b Oenological/winemaking practices

The Flavours

Although there are in excess of 250 million acres of grapevines planted on our planet, making it a substantial crop by any standards, when it comes to wine varieties two stand apart from the rest of the crowd. For red table wines, Cabernet Sauvignon is king; for white wine Chardonnay is, undisputedly, queen of the realm.

Personally, I find varietal Cabernets often boring, and sometimes downright unappealing. On the other hand, while some people don't necessarily like Chardonnay, it would be difficult to call it either of these things. It may not have the aromatic floral flavours of Riesling or Muscat, the spicyness of Gewürztraminer or the pungent vegetal character of Sauvignon (blanc), but I believe that Chardonnay makes the most complex varietal wines of all, ranging across the total flavour spectrum.

If there is anything in the winemaking world that is difficult to describe, the flavour of Chardonnay wins hands down, and by flavour I mean the combination of the senses of smell, touch and taste.

Smell is by far the most important of these three factors, enabling us to perceive odours from: the fruit/vineyard (figs. 1 & 1a); winemaking processes (fig. 1b); and maturation and evolution (fig. 1b).

The sense of touch is important for perceiving wine/body viscosity, oak and grape tannins, alcohol, and wine temperature. Most of these are inter-related and help make up the all-important structure of the wine.

Taste covers only the perception of the four basic taste stimulants: sugar (not sweetness), salt, acid and bitterness. As few wines these days are processed through ion exchange columns which convert potassium ions to sodium ions, salt is rarely a consideration in wine taste. Contrary to popular opinion, taste receptors (buds) are found over most of the oral cavity including the gums, lips, tongue and soft palate, but rarely on the top centre of the tongue or the hard palate – the roof of the mouth. An understanding of how our senses perceive the various signals sent by the wine will help us enjoy the nuances of each maker and vintage. However, rest assured that every person alive perceives these same signals in a different manner. This was amply demonstrated by a tasting I held where six of the best Champagne makers consistently saw opposing flavours in six wonderful bottles of bubbly or in the comparative Chardonnay tastings I conducted with wine professionals in London and Beaune.

The good, bad and great vintages of northern cold climates depend on happenings in the vineyard. Bad years are those of inclement weather and/or insufficient sunshine to bring the grapes to maturity. This can call for chaptalization (the addition of sugar to the fermenting must) which increases the alcohol levels, but does nothing for a wine's flavour, although it often improves its mouthfeel. Almost guaranteed sunshine and resultant full-ripeness on the east and west coasts of the USA, and in South America, Australia and New Zealand, provide the winemaker with a flying start; therein lies the difference in the basic flavours – as opposed to quality – of the wines from all these regions. (Chaptalization is illegal in all these countries with the exception of the American north-east.)

Vineyards in the colder regions of France, north-eastern USA, the northern area of the US west coast, Australia and New Zealand, yield grapes with aromas covered by the descriptive terms 'citrus', 'floral', 'melon', 'vegetal' (particularly in Chablis), 'herbaceous' and 'grassy' – see Fig. 1. Some clones of Chardonnay will produce pineapple flavours in the cold Carneros region south of Napa/Sonoma in California. It is worth pointing out that pineapple ranges from sharp, acid fresh, pineapple to sweet, canned pineapple. The canned flavour is more likely to be found in the warmer growing regions.

The stone fruit flavours of apricot, nectarine and peach are rarely, if ever, found in these regions being the hallmark of warmer viticultural districts. One line of thought regards stone fruit flavours as being associated with *Botrytis cinerea* or noble rot.

By observing Figs. 1, 1a and 1b the reader will be able to detect where the various flavours of Chardonnay originate. The fruit flavours, which are known as aroma, will give a reasonably accurate indication of the origin of the wine. 'Reasonably accurate' is important here. For while the citric and floral aromas are normally indicative of cold climate fruit, citrus is also the hallmark of Murray Tyrrell's wines from Australia's Hunter Valley. The explanation, as the man himself will tell you, is that the flavour is modified by the legal addition of citric acid. Just as it is legal, in some European countries, to add sugar where nature desists, some New World countries allow the addition of 'anything that comes from the grape itself' (acid, tannin or pigment, for example). 'Acid adjustment', to give the wine balance, is a common practice in warm, and not so warm areas.

The descriptors shown in Fig. 1b are known as 'bouquet' – the result of factors over which the winemaker has control. In varying amounts, these can increase in flavour perception. Listed on the left side are the sulphides which at low levels are very much complexing odours, but which at a smidgeon above those levels are unpleasant. At any perceivable level, professionals regard these as negative. These tend to be described as 'skunky', 'boiled cabbage', 'garlic' or 'burnt match' (sulphur) odours. Yeast flavours are variously described as 'burnt toast', 'toasty', 'biscuit' and a host of other yeast-related descriptors. The malolactic fermentation flavours start with dairy products such as cheese and butter and run to things like butterscotch; too much diacetyl can give a sour connotation. It is worth noting that diacetyl is the principal aroma of hazelnuts. Vanilla and smokey are derivatives of the oak, while the honey flavours so often mentioned around the world can come from gentle oxidation and any number of other winemaking, and possibly vineyard, practices.

The essential difference between ordinary, good and great Chardonnay, or any wine for that matter, can be summed up in three words: flavour, length and aftertaste. There is no doubt that wines possessing a balance of these three immediately stand out as great, within seconds of being taken into the mouth.

Length is the distance the flavour of a wine goes back in the mouth. A short wine will make an impression only in the front of the oral cavity (the mouth if you like) and the front part of the tongue, whereas a long wine will be mouth-filling and go all the way back to the throat. It's length and aftertaste that sorts the good from the great wines. Not only will a great wine have length from front to rear, but also a long aftertaste where the flavour of the wine lingers on. This means that the desirable fruity and complex flavours of the wine will still be evident in the mouth for as long as one or two minutes, or even more, after the wine has been swallowed. In addition, the acid level of the wine will be carefully balanced so that the mouth is left clean and fresh.

Chardonnay is essentially a food wine. When consumed without food it may appear to be a little too high in acid – sharp, tangy – but when enjoyed with a meal the mouth-cleansing of the acid will come into balance.

Tasting Chardonnay

If the Chardonnay lover is often confused, and even intimidated, by the multitude of flavours and winemaking practices from around the world, an even greater barrier is semantics. Frankly, the manner in which many words are used to describe wine, and the attributes that they are meant to cover, is laughable. Maybe these words mean something to you – or them – but do they mean the same to everybody? If ever we are going to appreciate and enjoy the subtleties of the multitude of Chardonnay flavours from the wineries of the world, it is vital that we learn to use meaningful words so that we can communicate with each other. It is not important that we agree about how we perceive the components of a given wine, but it is important that we are able to articulate and share our experiences.

To illustrate what I'm trying to convey to the reader, recently I asked winemakers from four countries to define five of the most commonly used words to describe wine flavour. Here are the words – and the answers:

(a) **Structure**
Respondent 1. How the wine is 'built'. All have a beginning, a middle and an end, in varying degrees.
Respondent 2. The feeling of the tannin and acid – how the wine holds together.
Respondent 3. Refers to a palate description, a summation of all the components of the palate which influence the final taste sensation.
Respondent 4. Body, strength (impression of durability). Concentration of flavour, enough of a wine's basic components (alcohol, acid, tannin) in balance.

(b) **Texture**
Respondent 1. Tactile sensation, viscosity and feel of the wine in the mouth.
Respondent 2. The feel of the wine – sugar, alcohol, glycerine, acid.
Respondent 3. A 'feel' sensation in the mouth – smooth, soft, thin, hard-middle and end sensations. Alcohol-tannin flavour concentration.
Respondent 4. Tactile impression in the mouth – oily, silky, astringent, harsh, etc. Texture or mouth-feel is a result of the amount of components; their balance (i.e. volume and interaction).

(c) **Mouth-feel**
Respondent 1. Same as texture.
Respondent 2. Same as texture.
Respondent 3. A combination of structure and texture – a term I use when talking about drinkability.
Respondent 4. I use these interchangeably.

(d) **Elegance**
Respondent 1. A romantic term not based on any particular sensory character, more a perception of style.

Respondent 2. (i) A polite way of saying that the wine is thin and lacks character.

(ii) Proper meaning: a wine with all aspects in harmony without being over-bearing or heavy or too strong. Body, intensity, acid-alcohol balance.

Respondent 3. A descriptor depicting some degree of class as determined by the winemaker – e.g. class of fruit and oak generally reserved for distinctive varietal styles and incorporating winemaking skills.

Respondent 4. Duration of balance. A sense of delicacy of balance, perfect balance, that carries through in the mouth from beginning to end. Balance and length.

(e) **Delicate**

Respondent 1. Euphemism for light.

Respondent 2. (i) Another polite way of saying 'not much there'.

(ii) Having faint intensity and light body, etc., but, *appropriate* to the whole wine – small and balanced.

Respondent 3. A suggestion of subtle 'hidden' flavours, nose and palate. 'Not an excuse for lack of flavour'. Young, immature wines lacking development in bottle.

Respondent 4. Often used to mean lighter flavour – I don't use it that way. Balance of textural components (alcohol, acid, tannin) in moderate intensity. Balance in high intensity would be 'rich'.

Having equipped ourselves with the terminology – let's put all this into practice and seek out the Chardonnays we like – and say why. By objective evaluation and opening one's mind to the plethora of new Chardonnays regularly appearing on retailers' shelves, there is a whole new world of wine sensations waiting, for one and all. Off to the wine shop with our shopping list which should comprise: a bottle each of California, Canadian, New York or any other eastern US state Chardonnay; maybe a South American (Chilean perhaps?); an Italian; Australian; New Zealand; and a Burgundy or three. Remember that at the bottom of the price range the wines we purchase will be fermented in stainless steel, possibly with a little oak maturation. So to find out the difference between that style and one that has been matured in oak we'll need to purchase either a Premier or Grand Cru Burgundy, or a top-class Pouilly Fuissé. Depending on your budget and the availability of these wines, one of the top California or Australian wines will suffice.

My shopping list would look something like this:

1. California – Robert Mondavi/Simi/Château St Jean
2. Canada – Château des Charmes/Inniskillan
3. France – Chablis – a choice of your own, maybe you have a favourite. (Need I say, be assured it's from Chablis)
4. Mâcon – Château de Dhamiry
5. Côte de Beaune – Puligny-Montrachet, Arthur Barolet et Fils
6. Pouilly Fuissé – Château de Fuissé
7. Italy – Antinori/Lungarotti/Tieffenbrunner
8. New York – Wagner
9. Australia – (a) stainless steel fermented – Wolf Blass/Seppelt/ Hardy Collection/Orlando. All these wines have had some oak cask maturation. (b) Barrel-fermented – Cullen's/Best's/ Tyrrell's/Rosemount/Leeuwin Estate/Petaluma
10. New Zealand – Cook's/Montana/Hunter's/Cloudy Bay

Since the London and Beaune Chardonnay events (see pages xxi–ii), it has been my policy not to conduct wine evaluations unless each of the participants had his or her taste thresholds measured. In this way it is possible to understand why some people say that a particular wine has too much acid, while others in the group say the same wine from the same bottle has too little. This happens in every tasting and comes about because each person has a different threshold for wine components, just as each person has a different set of fingerprints. If you are interested in determining each person's threshold for the various wine components you might care to make a copy of the record sheet used for the blanc de blancs tastings – see Figs. 2 and 3. To mix these solutions, preferably use distilled or very good quality water. For the acid solution mix two grams of tartaric or citric acid in a litre of water (the acid obtainable at your supermarket or home brew supplier), five grams of white sugar in a litre of water, and three measures of vodka in a little water will give you the right solutions.

Pour each person about two fluid ounces of each solution, which should be rolled around in the mouth and chewed, then spat out. Now give marks out of ten, according to where and at what strength you perceived the mixture. Note carefully the perception of the acid on the inside of the lips, gums and wherever. Acid gives wine *life*, sugar gives *body/viscosity* while alcohol provides *sweetness* and *viscosity*. Having tried each solution individually, now try

WINE EVALUATION RECORD

INTERNATIONAL WINE ACADEMY

Occasion _____

Place _____ Date _____

	WINE	PRICE	SIGHT 4 MAX	AROMA/ BOUQUET 6 MAX	IN MOUTH 6 MAX	AFTER-TASTE 3 MAX	OVERALL 2 MAX	TOTAL 20 MAX		FOOD PAIRING
1										
2										
3										
4										
5										
6										

Prior to Tasting

1. SIGHT

Appearance: Brilliant, star-bright, bright, clear, dull, cloudy, precipitated.

Colour: Colourless, very light/light/straw, straw green/light/medium/dark gold.
Pink, rose, light/purplish/medium/dark/tawny/brick red.

Saturation: Light, medium, deep.

Bubbles: Spritzig, size, quantity, rate, duration.

2. OLFACTORY

Aroma: Fruity, floral, spicey, vegetative, earthy.

Bouquet: Clean, fresh, dirty (H_2S, mercaptans, etc), yeasty, oak, SO_2, alcohol (no irritation).

Intensity: SO_2, alcohol (irritating).

In Mouth

3. GUSTATORY

Viscosity: Watery, thin, medium, full-bodied.

Taste: Sugar/sweet, bitter, sour.

Olfactory/flavor: Earthy, fruity, floral, herbaceous, woody, sweet, complex.

Tactile: Temperature, texture, irritation, gas.

Fig. 2

mixing the acid and sugar in equal portions and see if you can perceive both components, and as the solution has been considerably diluted see if the components have moved from the perception areas when tasted individually. You will note that the acid has given life to the sugar solution and the sugar has added viscosity to the acid. Now add the alcohol and see if you are able to identify each component and the part it plays in the blend.

If you are unable to measure grams, or your friendly pharmacist is not a wine lover (a very rare occurrence), just fiddle around in the

CHARDONNAY EVALUATION REPORT. NAME.................... WINE NO......

INTERNATIONAL WINE ACADEMY

Auckland, Melbourne, Singapore, San Francisco
P.O. Box 301, Malvern 3144
Australia

1 FRUIT
- ☐ Missing
- ☐ Identifiable
- ☐ Moderate
- ☐ Good
- ☐ Intense

Comments................

2. AROMA
- ☐ Floral
- ☐ Citrus
- ☐ Melon/Fig
- ☐ Honey
- ☐ Peach/Apricot

....

3. ACID
- ☐ Insufficient
- ☐ Moderate
- ☐ Balanced
- ☐ Coarse/Fine
- ☐ Excessive

....

4. EXTRACTIVES
- ☐ Light
- ☐ Moderate
- ☐ Coarse
- ☐ Balanced
- ☐ Excessive

Comments...............

5. YEAST
- ☐ Nil
- ☐ Evident
- ☐ Balanced
- ☐ Spicy
- ☐ Excessive

....

6. TECHNIQUE
- ☐ Clean
- ☐ Dirty
- ☐ Simple
- ☐ Well made
- ☐ Complex

....

7. COOPERAGE
- ☐ Concrete
- ☐ S/less steel
- ☐ Oak
- ☐ " toasted
- ☐ " charred

Comments...............

8. LENGTH
- ☐ Short
- ☐
- ☐ Medium
- ☐
- ☐ Long

....

9. AFTERTASTE
- ☐ Nothing
- ☐ Clean
- ☐ Short
- ☐ Medium
- ☐ Lingering

....

RATING

1. (Low)
2.
3.
4.
5.
6.
7. (High)

FOOD MATCHING

FISH
- ☐ Small
- ☐ Large
- ☐ Oysters
- ☐ Prawns
- ☐ Crab
- ☐ Lobster

MEAT
- ☐ Chicken
- ☐ Lamb
- ☐ Pork
- ☐ Veal
- ☐ Venison
- ☐ Beef

SAUCE
- ☐ Béchemel
- ☐ Butter
- ☐ Meunière
- ☐
- ☐
- ☐ Gravy

COOKING METHOD
- ☐ Steam/poach
- ☐ Pan fried
- ☐ Grilled
- ☐ BBQ
- ☐ Roast
- ☐ " rare/medium/well

Fig. 3

kitchen adding sugar and acid to the water until you are able to perceive the component in the solution. A word of warning – you need very little acid, yet more sugar than you think and you'll find them easier to mix in warm water. Now we should be able really to tear these wines apart! (Which is exactly what winetasting is *not* about! Always look for the positive factors in wine and not the negatives – there are already too many 'experts' doing that.)

Presuming that all the wines are of a similar vintage, bearing in mind that the southern hemisphere wines will be six months older, our first assessment will be the wines' colour. It would be surprising if the New World wines weren't showing more colour, owing to their riper fruit, which can be interpreted as more viscosity on the palate. Are the cold-climate Canadian, New York, California and Aussie wines deep in colour? These wines can also come from cold – very cold regions.

The study of wine colour is fascinating and can tell much about the wine. Now to the nose – the aroma and bouquet. Remember that, as a general rule, the aroma constitutes the flavours of the fruit and the bouquet represents those things that the winemaker has control over – sulphur dioxide, hydrogen sulphide, oak, yeast: the good and the bad things of winemaking.

A choice of two recording sheets is offered. Should you be using the Wine Evaluation Record (Fig. 2) follow the instructions beneath the chart. Alternatively, the Chardonnay Evaluation Record (Fig. 3) can be used; this I have designed specifically for Chardonnay tastings whereas the other is a multi-purpose sheet.

The nose: Fig. 3 tells us under 'Aroma' that Chardonnay can smell of anything from floral to peach/apricot while Figs. 1 and 1a provide the full spectrum of flavours. Generally speaking, the cold climate wines will have the floral and citric end of the smell range while the warm climate wines have the ripe fruit flavours of stone and tropical fruits.

Referring to Fig. 1b the taster will pick up bouquet factors and how the wine will taste in the mouth. The oak characters will be discernible by the vanilla and/or coconut flavours. If these and the yeasty characters which are noticeable as biscuit, toasty or just plain yeast flavours (having been a home ginger beer maker in my youth, I see both yeast and ginger flavours in 'sur-lies' wines) are too dominant, we can be assured that the wine is not yet ready to drink. Should these be integrated with the aroma of the fruit, we have a winner!

Of considerable importance is the fact that, unless a wine absolutely knocks you over with an outstandingly obvious aroma, few people perceive the aroma as one and the same thing. At a blanc de blancs tasting in Epernay for this book, the world's best Champagne makers saw a number of different aromas in the one wine – everything from spoiled by sulphur dioxide, through floral, biscuit, citrus and apple/pear. So don't feel intimidated if one person says that the Château de Chamirey smells like melon if you think it smells like pineapple.

PART TWO

Chardonnay Regions of the World

FRANCE

Burgundy

Chardonnay is grown in the four *départements* (counties, states) that constitute the Burgundy (Bourgogne) region: the Yonne (Chablis); the Côte d'Or, which includes the Côte de Nuits (almost exclusively a red wine region) and the Côte de Beaune, centred on the historic town of Beaune (including such well-known white wine names as Puligny, Chassagne and Meursault); the Saône-et-Loire (the *département* embracing the Côte Chalonnaise and the Mâconnais), which includes Mercurey, Rully, Givry and Montagny; and, finally, the Rhône – the *arrondissement* of Villefranche (while being in the Rhône *département*, it is technically part of Burgundy). Beaujolais represents almost half of Burgundy's vine area and red wine production, yet only about one per cent of this is Chardonnay, and that is almost all in the Pouilly Fuissé (Mâconnais) area, so it makes more sense to deal with it there.

The Institut National des Appellations d'Origine (INAO) has for fifty years tried to establish some law and order among the producers and distributors of wine in France. Their efforts have been followed, and in many cases copied, in most other European wine-producing nations. These laws are put into effect by appellation of origin controls – complex laws with far-reaching powers that have varying degrees of acceptance and success. Like all arbitrary laws, they are generally good and accepted; at times they are irritating and are ignored for nearly everyone's benefit. I said they were complex; that could be the understatement of the century, as they cover almost every aspect of production and sales. We can start by grouping these laws into four areas:

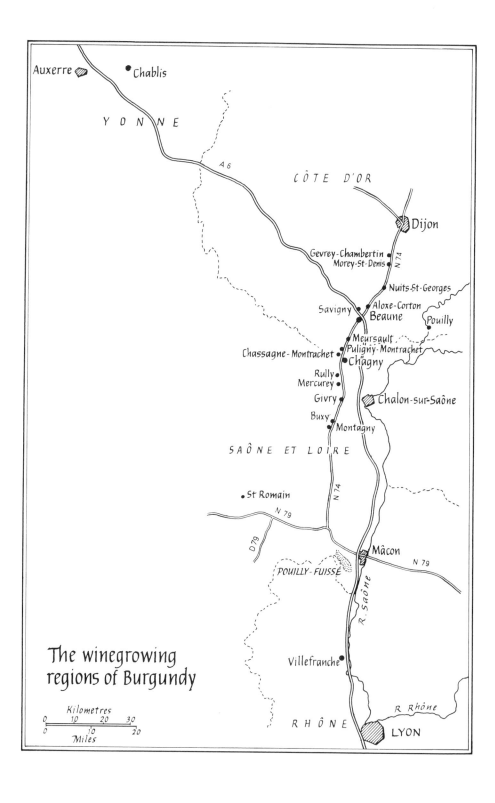

Auxerre   • Chablis

Y O N N E

A 6

CÔTE D'OR

Dijon

Gevrey-Chambertin
Morey-St-Denis

N 74

Nuits-St-Georges

Savigny   Aloxe-Corton
Beaune   Pouilly

Meursault
Chassagne-Montrachet •   Puligny-Montrachet
Chagny

Rully
Mercurey
Givry   Chalon-sur-Saône

Buxy
Montagny

S A Ô N E   E T   L O I R E

• St Romain

N 74

N 79

D 79

Mâcon
N 79

POUILLY-FUISSÉ

R. Saône

The winegrowing
regions of Burgundy

Villefranche •

R. Rhône

R H Ô N E   LYON

Kilometres
0   10   20   30
0   10   20
Miles

1. Vineyard production – listing specific areas where grapes can be grown. Unlike the freedom of choice in the New World, this is strictly defined. The laws also cover various cultural techniques including pruning methods (regardless of whether they are good or bad), and even declaration of stocks of wine held.
2. INAO specifies which grape varieties can and cannot be grown in a particular region. The essential difference between Burgundy and Bordeaux, with both red and white wines, is that Burgundy allows only one grape for each, Chardonnay for white and Pinot Noir for red wine. (There are secondary grapes, Aligoté for white wine and Gamay for red wine, but wines made entirely from these grapes must carry on the label Aligoté, Mâcon Rouge or Passetoutgrains.) In Bordeaux there are six red and three white varieties. It could be said that Burgundy wines are varietal, that is made from a majority of one grape variety, and those of Bordeaux, in the main, blended wines.
3. Maximum yield of grapes and wine from each hectare, a figure which varies from vineyard to vineyard, region to region, and sometimes year to year.
4. Minimum alcohol levels – this also varies from region to region and the wine classification within the appellation, e.g. a Grand Cru may require more alcohol than a Premier Cru, while a village wine will have an even lower minimum.

Burgundy alone has the staggering number of 114 different appellations. These can be enormously confusing: Chablis, for example, is the name of a town, a wine style (made entirely from Chardonnay) and an appellation. Grand Crus Chablis has an 11 per cent alcohol by volume minimum; the other Chablis classifications must be either a minimum of 9.5 or 10.5 per cent. The Chablis appellation enjoys the luxury of being able to chaptalize, without specific permission to bring their wines up to this minimum level. However, this is limited to 100 kilograms sugar per hectare and 2 per cent alcohol by volume. (For more information on chaptaliz-ation, see page 135.)

The Appellation Contrôlée laws also cover the wines from the grape stage to retail level. All wine despatched from the point of origin must be accompanied by an excise sheet, and, in the case of wholesalers and distributors, these particulars must be entered into a special receipt book. The retailer must also be able to support all purchases and sales with invoices and excise sheets.

CÔTE D'OR APPELLATIONS UNDER WHICH CHARDONNAY WINES MAY APPEAR ACCORDING TO AOC LEGISLATION

1 GENERAL AREA	2 SUB-COMMUNAL APPELLATIONS	3 COMMUNAL APPELLATIONS	4 PREMIERS CRUS APPELLATIONS	5 GRANDS CRUS APPELLATIONS	6 MINIMUM ALCOHOL (% ALC. VOL.)	7 MAXIMUM YIELD (HL/HA)	8 AVERAGE CHARDONNAY HARVEST (HL)
CÔTE DE NUITS	CÔTE DE NUITS VILLAGES				11.0	45	6
		FIXIN	FIXIN PREMIER CRU (10)		11.0 / 11.5	45 / 45	0
		MOREY-ST-DENIS	MOREY-ST-DENIS PREMIER CRU (20)		11.0 / 11.5	45 / 45	27
		VOUGEOT	VOUGEOT PREMIER CRU (4)		11.0 / 11.5	45 / 45	63
		NUITS or NUITS-ST-GEORGES	NUITS PREMIER CRU or NUITS-ST-GEORGES PREMIER CRU (42)		11.0 / 11.5	45 / 45	24
				MUSIGNY	12.0	40	7
CÔTE DE BEAUNE		LADOIX	LADOIX PREMIER CRU (7)		11.0 / 11.5	45 / 45	101
		ALOXE-CORTON	ALOXE-CORTON PREMIER CRU (15)		11.0 / 11.5	45 / 45	23
		PERNAND-VERGELESSES	PERNAND-VERGELESSES PREMIER CRU (5)		11.0 / 11.5	45 / 45	450
		SAVIGNY or SAVIGNY-LES-BEAUNE	SAVIGNY PREMIER CRU or SAVIGNY-LES-BEAUNE PREMIER CRU (22)		11.0 / 11.5	45 / 45	309
	CÔTE DE BEAUNE	CHOREY-LES-BEAUNE			11.0	45	12
		BEAUNE	BEAUNE PREMIER CRU (45)		11.0 / 11.5	45 / 45	123
		MONTHELIE	MONTHELIE PREMIER CRU (11)		11.0 / 11.5	45 / 45	541
		BUXEY-DURESSES	BUXEY-DURESSES PREMIER CRU (10)		11.0 / 11.5	45 / 45	59
							1,043

CÔTE DE BEAUNE	SAINT-ROMAIN			11.0	45	996

CÔTE DE BEAUNE						
	SAINT-ROMAIN			11.0	45	996
	MEURSAULT	MEURSAULT PREMIER CRU (25) MEURSAULT BLAGNY (4)		11.0 11.5 11.5	45 45 45	13,074
	PULIGNY-MONTRACHET	PULIGNY-MONTRACHET PREMIER CRU (23)		11.0 11.5	45 45	7,310
	CHASSAGNE-MONTRACHET	CHASSAGNE-MONTRACHET PREMIER CRU (54)		11.0 11.5	45 45	4,253
	SAINT-AUBIN	SAINT-AUBIN PREMIER CRU (29)		11.0 11.5	45 45	801
	SANTENAY	SANTENAY PREMIER CRU (16)		11.0 11.5	45 45	137
	CHEILLY-LES-MARANGES	CHEILLY-LES-MARANGES PREMIER CRU (3)		11.0 11.5	45 45	0
	DEZIZE-LES-MARANGES	DEZIZE-LES-MARANGES PREMIER CRU (1)		11.0 11.5	45 45	0
	SAMPIGNY-LES-MARANGES	SAMPIGNY-LES-MARANGES PREMIER CRU (2)		11.0 11.5	45 45	0
			CORTON	12.0	40	41
			CORTON-CHARLEMAGNE CHARLEMAGNE	12.0 12.0	40 40	1,168
			MONTRACHET	12.0	40	232
			CHEVALIER-MONTRACHET	12.0	40	174
			BATARD-MONTRACHET	11.5	40	398
			BIENVENUES-BATARD-MONTRACHET	11.5	40	119
			CRIOTS-BATARD-MONTRACHET	11.5	40	50

Fig. 4

All outlets, whether they be producer, wholesaler or retailer, are subject to inspection by INAO, the Service des Contributions Indirectes – a nice name for the taxman – and the Service de la Répression des Fraudes – or the fraud squad.

Labelling

Unlike the New World, where some may think that labelling laws are lax, Burgundy labels, despite their classic presentation, are a masterpiece of confusion for those of us who are not full-time students of the subject. It would be less than truthful if I said I understand them fully, but the chart of Côte d'Or appellations on pages 26 and 27 should enable you to do so.

By way of a fuller explanation, let us deal with each column in turn. Before we do so, it is worth noting that the appellation system is somewhat telescopic in nature. There is the overall **Burgundy** appellation; this descends to a more specific **commune** or town appellation; then there is a **climat** or a group of vineyards, and finally down to the 'cream of the crop', the specific vineyard appellations. As mentioned elsewhere, Burgundy differs from the New World, in that the best wines come from one vineyard. Invariably in the New World, where the winemaker is not hampered by AOC type legislation, the top wines are a blend of several vineyards.

The AOC communal wines (column 3) are those that embrace vineyards of a whole village and are not up to the previous two rankings, e.g. Mâcon, Beaune, Meursault. These are labelled 'Appellation [Name of Village] Contrôlee'.

In column 4 are the Premiers Crus, wines considered to be next in the pecking order after the Grands Crus and certainly a great place to start a fight about wine merits. Some should be there, some should be up, and others down the scale. The trouble is that when a grower gets into one of these slots there is just no movement, regardless of how good or bad the various vintages are. A label for this category might read: 'Mercurey Premier Cru' (in either upper or lower case) followed by the Appellation Contrôlée and often the actual vineyard name.

Column 5 lists the Grands Crus, *los supremos*: call them what you like but by some mystical method these particular appellations are regarded as the best. There is no question that many are good wines and there is also no question that there are other wines as good, if not better outside this ranking. But let's not argue here on what is best; that is another story, told in another place.

Examples of Grand Cru vineyards are Corton or Montrachet. Of course, the producer will hasten to add Grand Cru. Strangely, despite its international fame, no Meursault vineyard has made the top ranking; but the marketplace has spoken on this score. My own preference for Mercurey or Fuissé Chardonnay has not helped it move out of the Premier Cru category!

As far as possible, the details of column 6 are accurate. Columns 7 and 8 are a moveable feast. While the AOC laws are specific in both cases, they are also flexible in the event of a 'good' year. The local bodies (**syndicats**) or a specific grower can approach the authorities for permission to increase their production. Averages would indicate that these approaches are generally successful. The minimum alcohol level can be adjusted by chaptalization in a 'bad' year, but not more than 2 per cent.

Côte d'Or

The famous mustard city of Dijon sits like a proud queen at the northern end of both Burgundy and the 'golden slopes' of the Côte d'Or. Most of the fifty-four kilometres to the southern end of the region at the town of Chagny face the A6 autoroute which will take you either ski-ing in Switzerland, to the Mediterranean beach resorts of Cannes, Nice and Monte Carlo, or to the thirty-seven villages of the Côtes whose names read like a who's who of Burgundy wine.

The Côte d'Or is a complex wine *département*, even though only a small percentage (something like 2 per cent of available agricultural land) is devoted to viticulture. And to complicate things further, there are thousands of small growers with vine plantings averaging less than one hectare. This makes for a confusing picture, for all concerned.

In the hope of trying to guide the visitor to, or the buyer of, Burgundy, the first guideline is to forget all about what happens in any other vineyard area in the world. Burgundy is a whole new ball game. The small plots of land are the outcome of the French Revolution when the church and wealthy were dispossessed of their land which was then sold to entrepreneurs who dissected it into purchasable size parcels. In addition, the French laws of succession lay down that any land is equally divided between all the children, rather than the oldest. This has brought about a situation where Romanée-Conti Monopole vineyard is but one and four-fifths hectares, the *largest* single-owned vineyard in Meursault is three hectares and Puligny-Montrachet is four hectares. Compare this with the renowned Bordeaux châteaux of Lafite (eighty-eight hectares), Mouton-Rothschild (seventy hectares), Haut-Brion (sixty-six hectares), Latour (fifty-nine hectares) and Margaux (forty-two hectares).

Another indication of size can be found in Chablis where 1,200 growers between them own 880 hectares. These small holdings open the door for two singular features of the Burgundy wine scene – the *négociants* and the *co-opératives*.

The traditional role of the *négociant* seems to be ever-expanding. In days past they purchased, via brokers, wine from the many small growers (whose role we will examine further on), blended it (generally for improvement), bottled it and then marketed the finished product. These are the people who took Burgundy to the far corners of the earth and made it a household word; it even gave its name to a colour. Today their role includes buying grapes rather than wine and doing the job from start to finish. In many cases this has been brought about by the fact that the grower is just that – and not a winemaker. The skills required are different, just as they are for the specialist task of bottling wine. Due to the large volumes handled by the *négociants*/merchants, it is necessary for them to have people trained in each facet of production and for each of the wine styles, as these 'houses' will buy from every region of Burgundy, and some from many other regions outside of Burgundy. In all, there are over 150 such *négociants* based in the different towns of Burgundy, many with their own large vineyard holdings, from Chablis to Beaujolais. The Burgundy wine names likely to be encountered in your favourite wine shop will be one of these *négociants*. In their own particular way most will welcome you to their cellars.

The majority of the *négociants* can be found in Beaune and nearby Nuits St George; the balance are scattered through the small and large towns of Burgundy. The other large suppliers are the *caves co-opératives* (sometimes also called *un groupement de producteurs*), usually carrying the name of the town, although it is possible to find several groups in one town.

The essential difference between the *négociants* and the co-operatives is that the *négociants*' tasting facilities will offer the visitor wines from the whole Burgundy region (and will be available almost anywhere in the world), whereas the co-operatives will only offer local products. However, these co-operatives – generally large producers – are more than likely to supply 'buyer's own brand', the wines you find in your local supermarket or wine merchants with their own name on the label. The co-operatives represent excellent value for money, and besides some ordinary wine the prudent visitor is likely to find the odd 'gem'.

The bottom-line category of Burgundy producers is the domaine-bottled 'grower' – the one who grows the grapes, makes the wine and bottles the lot, or a portion. Unlike the producer elsewhere in the world, the Burgundy grower is likely to have a half hectare of vines in four or five appellations, bringing the fruit to the domaine for vinification.

Burgundy is an enormous magnet to wine lovers the world over, and while it attracts huge numbers of tourists the year round, the largest crowds come for the Hospices de Beaune charity auction in Beaune every November. This is when the Burgundy winemaker puts his 'babies' up for sale, and the rest of the world assembles to praise, which is often the case, or to pour scorn, as happens less frequently.

From the ring-road around the town of Beaune you can see many of the appellations, most of which are only a twenty-minute drive away. All these villages have excellent accommodation and even better restaurants. (Burgundy *is* wine and food: the hedonist's retreat!)

But it is here that the wine lover is also confronted with the evocative and esoteric terms so familiar to Burgundy and its wines – terms that are 'loose' and with little meaning to those not privileged to be in the inner sanctum of local knowledge or dogma. From a consumer's point of view, the Burgundy confusion starts when you walk into a wine shop to buy, say, a bottle of Meursault. And what do you find? Not one or two different brands of Meursault, but a whole host of appellations at incredibly different prices. As an example, a simple Meursault appellation will cost, say, $18, whereas a Meursault Charmes will be double the price at $35. What is the difference?

PULIGNY-MONTRACHET

APPELLATION CONTROLÉE

MIS EN BOUTEILLE PAR

JOSEPH DROUHIN

Maison fondée en 1880

NÉGOCIANT A BEAUNE, COTE-D'OR

AUX CELLIERS DES ROIS DE FRANCE ET DES DUCS DE BOURGOGNE

FRANCE 75 cl

One of the points to remember about white Burgundy is that the wines at the lower end of the price scale are almost certain to be fermented in stainless steel and, more than likely, to have had little or no new oak cask maturation. By way of example, the generic Joseph Drouhin Bourgogne blanc, which did so well in the Beaune tasting, was fermented in bulk in stainless steel whereas Drouhin's Grand Crus of Puligny-Montrachet and Premier Crus of Meursault will certainly be barrel-fermented.

Wines at the top end – the higher priced premiers crus and the grand crus – are, in most cases, likely to be barrel-fermented, using either old, new or mixed-age casks and priced accordingly. The value of these top appellations can be judged by a recent news release from Moillard, the largest Nuits St Georges shippers, who announced that they had purchased eight barrels of a particular wine in an appellation where they had no vines. To the distant observer, 200 cases of wine hardly merits a news release, yet, in Burgundy, the purchase of such gems is a coup.

Should our hapless purchaser buy a Meursault from an 'off' year, or a poor producer, that consumer is going to be very disillusioned by the rapid departure of those $35. Then there is the problem of multiple ownership of vineyards, such as Charmes, which can influence the quality of the wine. While it may all be one appellation, all Charmes are not born equal. Be assured, quality ranges from exceptional to shocking.

What devices does the consumer have at the point of purchase to guide him through the labyrinth of labels, besides personal experience or a knowledgeable wine merchant (and as the supermarkets take over wine retailing these are becoming rather thin on the ground)? Price counts for nothing. This was certainly reflected in the Burgundian's judging of their own wines in the Beaune event. The answer lies in a trip to this charming region – or in attending one of the many tastings held around the world.

Perhaps another way is to share the costs with half a dozen friends and conduct your own tasting. Having purchased a range of eight or so wines, go through them totally 'blind'. Cover the bottles with aluminium foil or a paper bag, and evaluate the wines without knowing their price or background. Preferably have a non-participant place the wines in order so that none of the tasters knows which is which.

Having tasted the wines once, taste them again to see if you can detect the characteristics for which the area is known – in the case of the Côte d'Or, the flavours include limey, citric, hazelnut and many others. Then see if you can detect the difference between the uncomplicated stainless steel ferments and the spicy, gingery characters of the '*sur-lies*' wines.

Only after constant practice will you be able to isolate the various flavour components you like and dislike. And remember, only *you* can determine what suits you best. By all means listen to what other people have to say, but don't feel intimidated by the 'know-all' (there's one in nearly every group).

There is no doubt that the Côte d'Or is the benchmark for this style of Chardonnay – but always be prepared for surprises, both good and less than ordinary. Quality varies enormously from one year to the next, and from one producer to another.

The Côte d'Or is divided into four distinct producing areas: the Côte de Nuits; the Hautes Côtes de Beaune and Hautes Côtes de Nuits; and the Côte de Beaune – or *the* place that is regarded as the essence of white Burgundy.

Of course, much white Burgundy comes from regions further south of the Côte d'Or and we'll come to that further on. In the meantime, let us take a trip through these better known areas.

Côte de Nuits

Even though white Burgundy is the proverbial drop in the bucket in this red wine empire, its few producers are serious about their labours. It is also here at Domaine Henri Gouges in Nuits St Georges that the wine lover can find the rarest of oddities; not Chardonnay but a wine made from the white mutation of Pinot Noir.

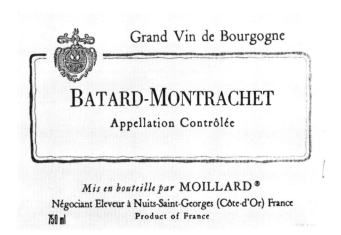

Grand Vin de Bourgogne

BATARD-MONTRACHET

Appellation Contrôlée

Mis en bouteille par MOILLARD®

Négociant Eleveur à Nuits-Saint-Georges (Côte-d'Or) France

750 ml   Product of France

Pinot Blanc, once thought to be Chardonnay, is another contributor to white wine in the Côte de Nuits region, and such a wine can be found at Domaine Ponsot in Morey St Denis and several other domaines. Compared with 23,000 dozen cases of red wine, Morey St Denis produces only 400 dozen white wine. It is a similar story at Musigny (100 dozen white as against 3,000 dozen red) and all along the Côte de Nuits. The visitor will also see some white wines from Clos Blanc de Clos Vougeot, and the vineyards of la Perrière and Clos Arlot. But white wine is scarce in this part of Burgundy so we will move on – southwards.

In Nuits St Georges can be found a number of merchants whose names are well known around the world, the biggest being Moillard and Faiveley, both with vineyards in the area. Some others are F. Chauvet, Geisweiler et Fils and Jean-Claude Boisset.

A word of warning – it is wise to telephone or write ahead to make appointments. For groups this is a necessity.

Hautes Côtes de Beaune and de Nuits

Maybe this is not the place for the Burgundy snob or purist, but it is certainly an interesting place to visit, high up above the autoroute. Because the high country means a colder region than the flat lands below which brings with it a later harvest, all sorts of viticultural experiments are taking place. In particular, they are experimenting with New World-style wide spacing between vines and high trellising as opposed to the traditional narrow rows and low vines.

These re-emerging Hautes regions are best known for Pinot Noir and Aligoté rather than Chardonnay; however I always find a visit to Les Caves des Hautes Côtes, Domaine Bernard Hudelot &

Verdel, Domaine Thevenot Le Brun, and Henri Naudin-Ferrand rewarding.

Côte de Beaune

Corton-Charlemagne provides a white wine more worthy than the original single name – Corton. Far removed from any other top white appellation, Corton-Charlemagne has its own band of followers who like the flinty yet spicy character of the wine. Often likened to Meursault, Corton-Charlemagne, with annual yields approximating 10,000 dozen, can be big and forceful in hot years. Many of the major *négociants* have a share of the action in this commune.

Five minutes away is Savigny-les-Beaune, more commonly referred to as Savigny, which produces about twenty times more red than white. This beautiful village is home to a number of good merchants and an unreasonable amount of Pinot Blanc. It is also the centre of sparkling wine production in this part of Burgundy. What a wonderful day it will be when there is enough Chardonnay to be used exclusively in Bourgogne Moussex!

Particularly in the United Kingdom, Swiss-owned wine giant and Savigny *négociant*, Henri de Villamont, is making remarkable headway with some excellent selections of white wine from around Burgundy. These are likely to be found under the labels of François Martenot or Arthur Barolet. Certainly worth a visit, as is Château de Corton-André in nearby Aloxe Corton.

A fascinating combination in Savigny is the almost wholly red wine property of Domaine Chandon de Briailles (relatives of Moët & Chandon). Among their eighteen hectares of red grapes, they have one-third of a hectare of white (equal proportions of Pinot Blanc and Chardonnay), mercifully vinified separately.

On the other side of the main road (N74) is Chorey-les-Beaune – not a Chardonnay community but where another value-for-money *négociant*, Domaine Tollot-Beaut, also handling a complete range of white Burgundy, can be found.

In the town of Beaune is an absolute smorgasbord of merchants presenting the entire gamut of Burgundy. Among the wine snobs, the giant Patriarche is not a fashionable name, but the firm offers excellent tasting facilities, even on Sundays, and a good white wine is not hard to find. Many of the fashionable houses are quartered in Beaune with their vast web of underground cellars. I often shudder to think what some of the buildings of Beaune are actually standing on – Chardonnay, Aligoté, Pinot Noir or solid earth? My guess would be not much of the last. The list of Beaune *négociants* is impressive: the two Bouchard firms, Joseph Drouhin, Jaboulet-Vercherre, Bichot, Jadot, Jaffelin, Louis Latour and a host of others. One locally produced wine of interest is the Chardonnay from the Lycée Viticole – the school of agriculture and viticulture.

Heading south and into the real target area we pass through the famous red wine villages of Pommard and Volnay, on to Monthelie where the traveller will find an almost unknown good value white at Charles Vienot. Among the other merchant/growers at Monthelie are Eric Boussey and Xavier Bouzerand. Then up the winding road, actually between the Côtes and the Hautes country, to St Romain, where for the first time the balance of red and white Burgundy is becoming something like equal before it tips completely in favour of white wine in the ensuing towns. Also at Saint-Romain is a very famous barrel-maker whose products are respected wherever wine is made. Domaine Germain Père et Fils, Domaine René Thevenin, Roland Thevenin et Fils, Armand Bazenet and Henri Buisson are certainly worth a visit.

Pressing on to the Montrachet country we find some famous Grand Crus vineyards are one half in Puligny and the other in Chassagne (the neighbouring town is Gamay, the name of the grape used in Beaujolais). Les Montrachet and Batard-Montrachet (which also completely embraces Bienvenues Batard-Montrachet) share a common boundary. The only vineyard which lies entirely in Chassagne is the minuscule Criots-Batard-Montrachet. It produces somewhere between 350 and 400 dozen cases of wine annually; for some reason, strong men become weak in their endeavours to obtain a case. The Grands and Premiers Crus of this area have been well documented in thousands of articles; it is perhaps the world's most discussed white wine. Of the reputed 'good stuff' there are but a few thousand cases to supply an international demand. Some of the well-known growers in Puligny are the Domaine Carillon Père et Fils, Domaine Leflaive, Domaine Etienne Sauzet, Domaine Jean Chartron, Domaine Henri Clerc et Fils, and the most recent-comer Olivier Leflaive. The list in Chassagne includes most of the well-known Beaune and Nuit St Georges houses, the Gagnard brothers, Delagrange-Bachelet, Domaine Marc Morey et Fils, Albert Morey et Fils and Ramonet-Prudhon.

Next door, almost, is the enigma of Burgundy – the great Meursault, without one Grand Cru. In many parts of the world, the hallowed name of Meursault is whispered in the same breath as Montrachet. Nearby, and included in any deliberations about Meursault, is Blagny which also butts up to Puligny. Meursault is the largest town on the Côte de Beaune and has a superb Château de Meursault well worth a visit (and a tasting); Robert Ampou et Fils, Domaine des Comtes Lafon (staggering Chardonnay!), Maison Jean Germain, Michelot-Buisson, Ropiteau Frères and Domaine Blagny are among a host of excellent merchants in Meursault and Blagny.

Undoubtedly, the wines of Montrachet and Meursault are expensive, and they are never ready to drink at the time of purchase, and may still not be ready for another decade. To my mind they are overpriced; after all, they don't come with a guarantee that they will be something out of this world.

However, there are other wines in this region that are not as expensive and are more readily drinkable. These come from the small local growers, which will either necessitate a visit to the area (though this can be an untrustworthy way to purchase wine – I get carried away with the people and the ambience!) or be bought from the major *négociants* under their *village* on Bourgogne blanc labels. The local co-operatives are also a wonderful source of value-for-money wines, even more so as we move south. As previously mentioned, many of the supermarkets buy wine to sell under their own labels and by watching the wine magazine tastings the alert buyer will pick-up the occasional bargain.

The United Kingdom is also well served by a unique group of people: the private wine consultant. These well-informed people visit France, and other parts of the world, regularly searching out bargains, and while few, if any, of them carry the popular supermarket brands, they normally have a range of exceptional value wines from around the world. Their services are highly recommended for the purchase of Burgundy wines.

Yonne

The region of Chablis, as opposed to the town of that name, is famous the world over for two main reasons. The first is that few other regions have had their name prostituted so persistently, to the point where there is now far more generic 'chablis' made around the world than is made in the region. The second is that someone has immortalized, with a poetic line, the rather strange notion that Chablis and oysters are welcome bed fellows.

Encouraged by the success of the Champenois crusade against the illegal use of their name, the Chablisiens are mounting an international campaign against those who seek to benefit from their lifelong toil. I do not believe that they have either the stamina or the muscle of the Champenois necessary to succeed. One of the major problems in this Chablis argument is that New World 'chablis' – whether from California, New Zealand or Australia – is not made from the expensive Chardonnay grape, nor is it grown in the same cold climate. In fact, as a general rule, the opposite applies – cheap grapes and hot climates, often with a fair degree of sweetness.

A couple of oddities about the region of Chablis concern the co-operative which produces more than one-third of all local wines for its 190 members. They bring the pressed juice (or 'must') to the winery where it is made into wine for eventual sale, either under the co-operative label (La Chablisienne) or that of each individual member, who come from each of the twenty communes and represent everything from Grand Crus to Petit Chablis. (Petit Chablis is the lowest classification of wine, coming from the outlying areas and is mainly consumed locally.) A masterpiece of organization to some, but confusion to those of us not intimately familiar with the region's wines.

At the end of the 1980s, Chablis is at the vinous crossroads, having survived one crisis after another during its long history. Styles are changing; there is more new oak cask fermentation and maturation nowadays, and only the most loyal follower appears to to prepared to ride out the rapidly changing scene. Due to its unfavourable location, the region is cursed with terrible weather, and while it remains on many restaurant wine lists in Europe and the UK, at the prices being asked the New World is turning more to Burgundy and its own products.

Yet the question remains: what is Chablis? Stylistically, it is the full spread of everything that can be done to a grape – from 100 per cent stainless steel fermentation to the extremes of new oak

RÉCOLTE DU DOMAINE

CHABLIS

APPELLATION CONTROLÉE

MIS EN BOUTEILLE PAR

JOSEPH DROUHIN

Maison fondée en 1880

NÉGOCIANT A BEAUNE, COTE-D'OR

AUX CELLIERS DES ROIS DE FRANCE ET DES DUCS DE BOURGOGNE

FRANCE   75 cl

vinification. Between these stylistic phenomena of black and white, the shades of grey alter dramatically to the extent that there must be lots of consumers who are thoroughly confused – and disappointed. In many ways, there is not a lot of difference between the average Chablis and Coteaux Champenoise, you either like them or you don't; it is a very personal thing. It has not been my good pleasure to drink a great bottle of Chablis at its peak; not many people have. But I still find it a fascinating exercise to taste, side by side, a bottle of unwooded, say, Domaine Jean Durup, a bottle of balanced oak maturation – try Domaine Philippe Testut – and the new oak style of 'the king' Domaine William Fevre! A very educational experience which will provide a tour of Chablis in ten minutes!

Although half of the Chablis production is handled 'out-of-town' by Beaune merchants, the region is well served by merchants in the various villages and towns of the Yonne. Coming quickly to mind are: Domaine Laroche, the Cave Co-opérative la Chablisienne, Domaine Pinson, A. Ragnard, René Dauvissat, Jean-Paul Droin, and Louis Michel et Fils.

Côte Chalonnaise

A remarkably scenic area stretching from Rully in the north to Montagny in the south, embracing the appellations of Rully, Mercurey, Givry and Montagny. An autumn drive through the region at vintage time, even on a bicycle, is both hazardous and enjoyable. The route was pioneered more than 1,000 years ago when a horse and rider travelling in opposite directions constituted a traffic jam. Nowadays, at vintage time the horses are gone, being replaced by mechanical grape harvesters and large tractors hauling trailer-loads of grapes to the *cuverie*. Try negotiating these in what are now mini-canyons between the houses, as you take in this page of history and the super scenery – it is exciting!

In total, the Mercurey region represents sixteen per cent of overall Burgundy production, only ten per cent of this figure being Chardonnay. This tiny 1.6 per cent of Burgundy's Chardonnay should not be lightly dismissed. In fact, when I look for a good Chardonnay in France (and by that I mean a value-for-money wine) my sights automatically zero in on Mercurey or Fuissé. As yet this southern part of Burgundy, with rare exceptions, is not privy to the general razzle-dazzle and hype that is such a feature of the marketing and promotion of Beaujolais and the Côte d'Or.

Aligoté, the second white grape of Burgundy, represents a

similar amount to Chardonnay, much of it being used in Crémant de Bourgogne, the increasingly popular Champagne look-alike. Most Crémants are made by the *méthode champenoise*, and many growers are reducing the Aligoté content in favour of Chardonnay. My fossicking through the tiny villages from the south to the north of Burgundy in search of truly varietal 100 per cent Chardonnay was unsuccessful. No doubt there are many of them, but I couldn't find one. The impression I have formed about Crémant de Bourgogne is that the blanc de noir (white wine made from black grapes) is in many ways superior to the wine made from white grapes (blanc de blancs). I do not think that the latter will ever be a force until it is 100 per cent Chardonnay. Having said that, it does not mean for one second that Crémant is not good 'fizz'; it certainly isn't Champagne, but then neither are the prices! Much wine comes from other areas of Burgundy to be made into sparkling wine, a specialist business if done properly, then returned to the owners in distant places who, in turn, sell it under their own label. This process is called contract making and bottling.

Rully and André Delorme are synonymous with Crémant de Bourgogne and any number of other excellent regional wines. The present-day winemaker/proprietor, Jean-François Delorme, one-time Mayor of Rully, is one of the great characters of Burgundy. Also in Rully the wine lover will find other good merchants in Jean-Claude Brelière and Domaine Ninot Rigaud.

Snug up against the Rully vineyards are those of Mercurey, one of my favourite places even if red wine outnumbers white at the outrageous odds of 20:1. It is certainly an area with a high degree of winemaking technology which shows in the end products. The wines of Antonin Rodet, Michel Juillot and Château de Chamirey in particular are as well made and flavoursome as any in Burgundy. Confusing because of the similarity in name, Château de Chamilly also offers excellent value.

Onwards to Givry where the imbalance of red and white persists, yet here one can find some excellent value whites – not a lot but worth the search. Try Jean Cleau, Domaine Ragot and Jean Chofflet, I don't think you will be disappointed. Last, and certainly not least, is Buxy and its now famous co-operative with its tasting cellar situated right on the main corner of the town. The simple unwooded Montagny des Caves is a wine that can be enjoyed some years after bottling. The most recent vintages have had a touch of new oak and are really quite something. Of course there are other labels besides Montagny at the co-operative well worth tasting.

All the vineyards of Montagny can use the Premier Cru appellation, maybe this isn't wise but this is a decision for you, the buyer, to make after tasting. Château de la Saule is a popular favourite amongst 'those in the know', while Jean Vachet also has a strong following. Good wines are easily obtained in Buxy.

Mâconnais

Among the six appellations of this region, Chardonnay is king, making up slightly more than an impressive two-thirds of the Mâconnais' 250,000 litre production. The Mâconnais and the Côte d'Or each represent 35 per cent of Chardonnay production in Burgundy.

Here you can savour some of the Chardonnays that have added so much lustre to the fascination of Burgundy. At the southern end, the twin villages of Fuissé and Pouilly are linked together in the appellation of Pouilly-Fuissé, along with Chaintre, Solutre and Vergisson. This is a rather awe-inspiring area with vines on all sides, up and down the mixed soil slopes dominated by the breakaway Solutre and Vergisson ridges. For those interested in a touch of history with their wine, these spectacular outcrops are full of wonderful tales.

Even if the scenery, vineyards, culture and food are terrific, it is the wines of the region that are most legendary. And not without reason. It has been my good fortune to taste, judge and evaluate countless Burgundy wines, and I find them a mixed bag. But here, particularly in Fuissé, I think Burgundy hits its peak, with all the possible flavours of Chardonnay, at reasonable prices. Of course, as in every other Burgundy region, the top wines cost a fortune it seems; yet I have no trouble in the value-for-money department here. To me, the Château de Fuissé,with its several labels, is a knock-out. Put the top wine, Château Fuissé, in your mouth and you know you have a wine with lots to say. None of those funny 'elegant' or 'delicate' quotes about this wine; this is *real* Wine with a capital W. Château de Beauregard, Louis Curveaux, Gilles Noblet and Roger Luquet can also be relied on to provide excellent wines.

However, all over the Mâconnais, with 85 per cent of the Chardonnay being produced by co-operatives, there are good wines at reasonble prices just waiting to be found.

Among these the Caves Co-opératives at Chaintre is the largest producer of Pouilly-Fuissé; it together with the neighbouring Vinzelles Co-operative are certainly places to fill most needs. While visiting Chaintre, don't miss a tasting visit to the Château de Chaintre. The village of Saint-Veran with its tiny appellation is attracting attention among wine lovers and several good producers can be found there. Try the co-operative, the Maison Mâconnaise, also Producteurs de Prisse. Another small town making a big reputation is Davaye where you will find recommended suppliers in André Corsin, Henry-Lucius Gregore and the Lycée Agricole. It makes a fascinating study going from one town to another and comparing the styles and philosophies of the wines made from the same grape. Of course, this difference can be found in every wine village the world over, but it seems more fun here! As we head north, travelling from one village to another is little problem in the Mâconnais. So many other wine regions around the world would do well to copy the wonderful sign-posting of the Route des Vins Mâconnais-Beaujolais – top places to take a picture for the family album!

Between the roads D89 and N79 is Charney-les-Mâcon, where the well-known merchant Mommesin and the lesser known Trenel Fils dispense some good bottles, while at Levigny can be found Domaine Maciet-Poncet – all worthy of your visit.

The wines of Mâcon Villages – which might also carry the confusing but legal label Pinot-Chardonnay-Mâcon (wines can be easily misunderstood) – certainly aren't all great. Yet the forty-three villages are worth exploring and one is certain to find something to suit. Mâcon-Lugny is the village where the unusual Chardonnay Musque seems to thrive. It can certainly provide a flowery and, in many cases, a real 'muscaty' flavour to the wine. A visit to the Lugny Co-operative can be quite an educational experience.

Naturally, no visit to Burgundy for the Chardonnay lover is complete without going to the tiny village of Chardonnay. Yes, there is such a place where one can sit in the café or stand at the Co-operative and ponder if this is the village that started a modern-day wine revolution!

By the way, Mâcon Supérieur is a quaint way of saying the wine has an extra one per cent alcohol.

Champagne

Champagne is the drink of happiness and celebration. In view of the amount consumed around the globe, it continues to surprise me that few people know that Champagne is made from two-thirds red/black grapes and one-third Chardonnay.

As this book is about Chardonnay, the Champagne content will be limited to blanc de blancs (white wine from 100 per cent white grapes) and Coteaux Champenois – or 'blanc tranquilles' as the still white wine is known in the region. Both are made exclusively from Chardonnay grapes.

There is an old story concerning the irrepressible Noël Coward who was interviewed on arrival in New York. When asked by reporters if it was true that he had a bottle of Champagne for breakfast every morning, his surprised answer was, 'Doesn't everybody?' I've fully endorsed that viewpoint for three decades. I am not known as 'Champagne Al' for nothing.

Champagne has many uses, not the least being the launching of boats of all sizes, celebrating a victory, a marriage (or does that come under victories?) or a birth.

In what is possibly the coldest wine-producing region and among the most northerly vineyards in the world (only the earliest ripening black Pinot and Chardonnay will ripen here) countless folk tales have compounded and become part of the fascination of this superb beverage. Many of these tales revolve around the legendary figure of the man who was reputedly the creator of Champagne, the blind monk Dom Pérignon.

Moët & Chandon must be commended for the superb manner in which they have preserved the Hautvillers Abbey, pouring millions of francs into its restoration and maintenance, and into researching the historical aspects of the man and his work. Included among the Abbey's treasures is one of the few identifiable contacts with the monk, the monastic Order's books of accounts signed by the man himself, including a signature in the year of his

death. (Many scholars will say that this is not the signature of a blind man.)

One of the sad factors relating to the turmoil of French history over the centuries is the almost continual devastation of life and property. Besides the French Revolution, there was the 100 Years War and two World Wars, all of which raged through the Champagne region destroying almost every historical record.

It is only by the careful sifting of snippets of information and by matching stone, wood and metalwork against known classic pieces that one can determine whether particular pieces of memorabilia – or certain tales – are true or false. And Champagne has its share of both. Unfortunately, the real truth behind the Dom Pérignon mystery may never be known despite Moët & Chandon's unselfish contribution in the way of research, and the employment of motivated people.

Yet another question mark hovers over the exact part the monk played in the Abbey and the making of wine. While it is known that many people came to the Abbey to taste 'the wines of Dom Pérignon', his true role was that of business manager/accountant (as the position would be known today). Brother Pierre was, in fact, the viticulturist and, possibly, the true originator of the white wine from red/black grapes. Until the time of the monk and the Brother, it is almost certain that all Hautvillers, if not all Champagne, wine was red.

In no way am I trying to make a case against Dom Pérignon's work or contribution, but it is important to recognize that wine-making represented only a small part of the Abbey's overall farming business and religious participation.

By experimentation, accident or otherwise (most advances in viticulture/oenology seem to fall into the latter two categories), Brother Pierre observed that the grapes harvested before 10 a.m. did not pick up the red colouring from the skin and produced a white juice from red/black grapes when crushed. (I say red/black because to say one or the other is confusing in that the grape's name is black Pinot (noir) yet it makes red wine.) Once this incredible achievement had been assimilated, a new winemaking chapter was opened – blanc de noirs, or white wine from black grapes.

However, blanc de blancs Champagne – not blancs tranquilles, the still wine made from 100 per cent Chardonnay – is relatively new on the Champagne scene. It is terribly fashionable of late, even if the people who like the sound of those magic words have very little idea of their meaning. Yet Moët & Chandon, by miles the largest Champagne house, doesn't even make such a product, nor will they move from their position that Champagne, any Champagne, can only be made by blending. And this applies to their blancs tranquilles, Saran, too, which is a cross-blend of regions and vintages. They say that complexity and consistency come only from blending the two Pinots (Noir and Meunier) with Chardonnay: their 1911 blended Champagne is still in perfect condition, they will tell you, while some of the 1973 vintage blanc de blancs have fallen to pieces. The Moët philosophy demands a consistency that they say is unavailable from any one grape variety, although Moët have a sister company, Dom Ruinart, who do make a blanc de blancs.

La Champagne (the Champagne region) has two distinct Chardonnay-growing areas: the first is the east-facing Montagne de Reims to the north which, the locals say, produces grapes with more fruit and body. The people who will vociferously oppose that proposition are growers from the other chief growing area, along the Côtes des Blancs, south of Epernay, where the grapes are said to be more floral scented. This area, which includes the delightful little villages of Cramant, Oger, Avize and Mesnil-sur-Oger, has recognized claims to fame in providing Champagne with its most sought-after and expensive grapes. And the most stunning of all vineyard scenery. This east-facing view is an interesting anomaly: the Côtes defy the traditional policy of having vineyards face south to obtain maximum benefit from the sun. Chardonnay from the Côtes des Blancs is the cornerstone of the Champagne blend, providing freshness and length, and in the blend encouraging other wines to sparkle easily – or *prendre la mousse*, as they say.

The normal run of Champagne is made from a blend of three grapes, Pinot Noir, Pinot Meunier and Chardonnay. Pinot Noir is said to give body, while Pinot Meunier is responsible for fruitiness (see figure 5). The Champagne 'purists' condescendingly consume blanc de blancs for its lightness and as an apéritif, but claim that it is not 'real' Champagne. What rot! On the other hand, blanc de noirs (white from black) is almost unknown in France but a hot item in the USA.

There is a story on the Côtes des Blancs that all their blanc de blancs does, in fact, contain some Pinot Noir, maybe 10 per cent, to provide a little body. One man who contests this very strongly is Christian Pol Roger who steadfastly maintains that blanc de blancs *is* white wine from white grapes – it is either blanc de blancs or it isn't. If it contains any red grapes it is not, and cannot be, blanc de blancs.

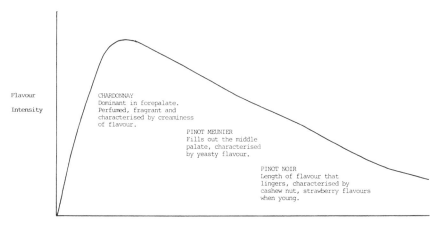

Fig. 5   Palate structure: champagne

Another wine of considerable interest from the Côtes in particular, but Champagne generally, is the appellation Coteaux Champenois still white wine, the great 'medicine' of Brother Pierre. This wine does not have many adherents in the wine-consuming world, it being very acid and fresh with little varietal character. Yet I have enjoyed this wine with local food and found it extremely pleasant, which is, really, what wine is all about – the marriage with good food.

As a general rule, the consumer seems to be totally confused about the division and duties of grapegrowers and winemakers in Champagne. The following statistics, kindly supplied by the Comité Interprofessionel du Vin de Champagne portray an

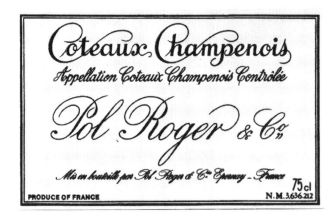

excellent example of the ratio of grapegrowers to winemakers. The total number of grapegrowers in the Champagne appellation is 15,000, while the number of producers of Champagne is a fairly hefty 5,200. The number that makes blanc de blancs is somewhere between 800–900 while about 250 make Coteaux Champenois. The last two figures are approximate.

Other Regions of France

Just like Italy, the business of the French grower being tied down by laws as to what he can and can't grow is becoming a bit of a bind. As Chardonnay is a hot number in the markets of the world, growers in both countries want to get their share of the action. And, certainly, Chardonnay *can* produce more reliable, and in my opinion, better fruit in areas other than Burgundy. Efforts to date have not proven my hypothesis but I think this is a philosophical rather than a practical one.

Let's take the rather bold example of Louis Latour's expedition into the Ardèche, where a tremendous commitment has been made. The firm has shown enormous initiative, albeit commercially motivated, to satisfy the world's demand for Chardonnay, but it appears on the surface that they are equally determined that the Ardèche wine will not equal or surpass their Burgundy efforts. Fair enough, these are early days – maybe the vines are young – but I have little doubt in my mind that a winemaker from the New World could make a far more acceptable wine from this fruit. Not unlike a newspaper which can show any face of a public identity to suit their purposes – happy, generous, passionate or scowling – a winemaker can do the same thing to wine. It was often said by my tutor that you can easily tell what a wine is like, simply by looking at the maker's face! I've not yet seen Monsieur Latour so I can't comment on his countenance.

The one planting of Chardonnay in France that really thrills me is the one in Bergerac. 'Chardonnay in Bordeaux?' you might say, 'You must be joking!' Not really; admittedly it's microscopic in size, but the outcome will be interesting.

In the Jura, up there on the high country near the Swiss border, Chardonnay is an important part of life, despite the inhabitants' approach to classic winemaking. It could be said that most Chardonnay drinkers would dramatically go off the variety (and maybe wine altogether), if they had to drink Chardonnay from the Jura. It is different, very different, but certainly worth trying so that one can formulate one's own opinion.

Chardonnay is not new to the Loire, but up to this time please spare me the endeavours. Once again, though, it's early days and it *is* an area worth monitoring.

Of intense interest, to me anyhow, are the endeavours in the south; Minervois in particular. That wonderful stretch of Mediterranean country between Montpellier and the Spanish border is ripe for making the classic styles of the New World. At the moment they are all fairly ordinary country wines, but this is a price-sensitive approach. Hopefully, we will see some forward-thinking and artistic people pick up the ball and run with it; quality is, after all, in the mind.

NORTH AMERICA

D ue to its large number of native vines, North America was named 'Vineland' many hundreds of years ago by the earliest explorers along the Atlantic coast.

The first settlers brought their own vines from Europe, but the vines all perished from some strange malady within a few years. They would not grow even for Thomas Jefferson, the third US President, ardent wine enthusiast and writer, who, for over thirty years tried in vain to persuade them at his Monticello home, Virginia. Throughout his life, Jefferson, who had a superb cellar of wine, exhorted his fellow Americans to grow and drink wine with such historic lines as 'No nation is drunken where the wine is cheap; and none sober where the dearness of wine substitutes ardent spirits as the common beverage.'

What killed the vines was possibly America's only unwanted gifts to viticulture – four pests and diseases that rocked the foundations of winegrowing throughout the world. In their own homeland, among their own vines, these maladies were harmless; but when let loose among the tender European vines they were a disaster.

As American vine cuttings were taken to Europe for breeding purposes, so were powdery mildew (*c.* 1852), black rot (*c.* 1855), the root louse phylloxera (*c.* 1863) and downy mildew (*c.* 1878). The famous Bordeaux mixture, still used in gardens and vineyards the world over, coped with powdery mildew but nothing short of completely uprooting the vines was effective against phylloxera. Europe, and most of the rest of the world's vineyards, including California's, were annihilated.

So for many years Eastern American wine was made from the native varieties which flourished and produced some excellent Champagne and fortified wine styles. But they had a strange flavour for table wines, and were generally not liked by those who had a taste for European grape wines. It was the cure for phylloxera (as explained in the Rootstocks chapter, page 140) that changed all this. The rootstocks came from such unlikely places as Missouri and Texas. This discovery made the growing of the European varieties possible in North America (and the rest of the world), although, until nearly a century later, the eastern states and Canada had the problem of cold weather adaptability. A continent the size of North America presents many problems to the farmer.

Not a well-known fact is that the California and South American wine industries had their roots in Mexico and, while grapegrowing and winemaking flourishes in the former Spanish colony to this day, Chardonnay is not a factor in Mexico – yet.

While Chardonnay was known in California as early as the turn of the century, it was ignored until the 1950s and was almost unknown in any other part of the country until the late 1960s. Nowadays, the wine lover can do what President Jefferson had hoped for 170 years ago, sample a Virginian Chardonnay of world class, or perhaps one from Texas, New York, Michigan or wherever.

As for California, well, their Chardonnays are just about the best there is. In fact, they make the best California Chardonnays in the world!

California

Taking the line that Chardonnay and white Burgundy are different animals, California, for more reasons than one can count, is the Chardonnay centre of the world. Chardonnay *per se* could, in fact, be considered as a California wine style if we accept that Chablis is Chablis and Meursault its own thing rather than varietal Chardonnay.

Larry Walker, San Francisco wine columnist and managing editor of the influential trade magazine *Wines and Vines*, says that there are two categories of California Chardonnays. The first is inexpensive (under $5) cold fermented and showing little varietal character – almost a generic wine with a little sweetness on the finish. The second, which is the more serious Chardonnay category, contains a greater variety of wines, with greater emphasis on oak and the Chardonnay fruit character.

Phil Hiaring Jnr, editor of *Wines and Vines*, said that in years past

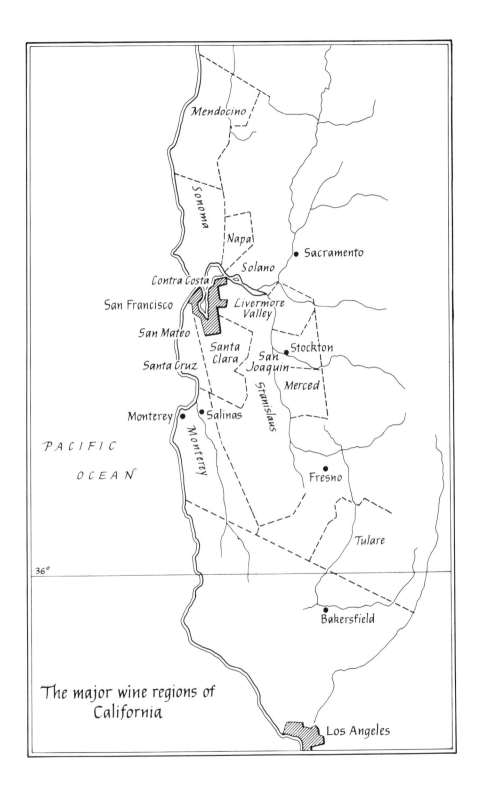

Mendocino

Sonoma

Napa

Solano

• Sacramento

Contra Costa

San Francisco

Livermore
Valley

San Mateo

Santa Cruz

Santa
Clara

San
Joaquin

• Stockton

Merced

Stanislaus

Monterey

• Salinas

Monterey

PACIFIC

OCEAN

Fresno

36°

Tulare

•
Bakersfield

The major wine regions of
California

Los Angeles

a California Chardonnay priced at under $5 was considered, on price alone, to be no good. Only high-priced wines from small producers were considered worthy. Not so five years later when the bulk of sales, despite inflation, are in that price range. He says that there was an over-kill with oak (during the 1970s) and that California winemakers got it 'screwed-up' thinking that the Burgundians used all new oak when, in fact, they (the Burgundians) picked up the technique from the Californians! 'Some people would hoot you out of the stadium if you said we are moving towards food wines – but I think that's the way we're going, and not only with Chardonnay. When you have a meal you don't want the wine to dominate the food – well, I don't anyhow,' says Hiaring.

California Styles

California has Chardonnay growing in twenty-two counties, covering a 1988 total bordering on 30,000 acres. This is double the amount planted in Burgundy. The fruit from these regions, in most cases, provides a different flavour base for the winemaker, which accounts for the careful regional and vineyard selection by the state's leading winemakers. It also points up the essential difference between the freedom enjoyed by California winemakers and those of Burgundy who are subject to strict appellation limitations. The longer Chardonnay is made in the northern hemisphere, the more California and Burgundy wines will be compared – a futile and useless exercise. Some California Chardonnays might be like, or even mistaken for, Burgundy wines; maybe some people are deliberately trying to copy the French style. But, in my opinion, these winemakers are denying the consumer the true local flavour and also something which is uniquely Californian.

An interesting facet of Chardonnay in California is that most, if not all, makers have at least two classes of Chardonnay, normally referred to as 'regular' and 'reserve'. Most have more than two categories; three or four grades are not uncommon and I even found one producer with eight different Chardonnays. What is the difference between 'regular' and 'reserve', or the other host of sophisticated names that the marketing men hang on these unsuspecting wines? Simi Wines in Sonoma circulate an excellent *Simi News* periodical and their Volume 4, No. 1, issue gives a precise definition of their styles which, I believe, could apply to most other wineries, almost anywhere in the USA:

Our regular release emphasises fruit. We want a subtle mix of aromas in the nose, a pleasantly round and delicate mouthfeel with full flavours, and a long, smooth finish. Our style objectives for the reserve Chardonnays emphasise power and intensity. Their aromas emphasise sweet, toasted oak. The fruit is both spicier and more complex. In the mouth, these wines are rich without excess weight. We select what we anticipate will be the most intensely-flavoured grapes. These are generally barrel fermented in new French oak and aged on their fermentation lees. They do not age much longer in oak than the regular Chardonnays. Final selection and blending of reserve components is done just before bottling, then the wines receive two years bottle ageing at the winery before release.

Wine styles, even within a small appellation, can vary wildly. In a state the size of California there are countless ever-changing styles. Generally, it would appear that the 'block-buster' styles of the 1970s have gone, even though many lovers of the big oak flavour are having severe withdrawal symptoms or have changed brands to makers continuing this style.

In the late 1980s the preferred style among the *cognoscenti* is one with lower alcohol levels, less and better balanced oak, more Chardonnay fruit flavour, wines that are drinkable sooner but that also will live longer without falling to pieces in their comparative youth. In some quarters these are called 'elegant', a term with a million meanings to a million people, but one to be wary of. (My interpretation of elegant is a wine lacking in body/viscosity – see page 9, 'The Flavours', for other definitions.)

The enormous University of California, at its Davis campus just a few miles west of the state capital, Sacramento, has been the force behind California's pre-eminence with Chardonnay. It is there that the many vine clones, now successfully used throughout the New World, have been developed from the one 'mother' vine. UC Davis has contributed even more in wine research and the training of winemakers who have gone on to incredible heights of artistic expression, particularly with this variety.

So many of the Davis faculty are associated with all aspects of wine production, from the importance of oak-ageing to sensory evaluation, that it would be unfair to single out one or two names from such a long list. However, I believe that the international work of one person, Professor Harold Olmo, in the field of vine breeding will always be associated with Chardonnay and UC Davis.

Still, the clonal breeding work is not without its critics. More than a few vinegrowers think that the heat treating, and consequent 'cleaning-up' of the viruses that affect vine growth, also have a negative affect on grape quality in terms of flavour. The virus-free Curtis clones, as they are known, yield somewhere near double the amount of grapes as the untreated Wente clones. This is great for the grapegrower who is paid by the number of tons of grapes delivered to the winery with specific acid and sugar levels, but when it comes to the old-fashioned 'berry in the mouth' taste test, the virused low-yielding clones appear to deliver the greater flavour.

A book of this nature will, unintentionally and despite efforts to the contrary, ruffle the feathers of quite a few people by failing to mention new areas and producers of merit. While every effort has been made to cover the global plantings of Chardonnay, there have been some limitations imposed by time and money. On the other hand, despite extensive plantings of Chardonnay throughout the Golden State, the centre of Chardonnay production and expertise (with few notable exceptions) is surely located in the Sonoma Valley (8,000 acres), to a slightly lesser extent, the Napa Valley (7,300 acres) and, more specifically in the Carneros region which is located in both Napa and Sonoma counties. I repeat that there are some notable exceptions, these occurring from Mendocino (2,150 acres) in the north to Santa Barbara (2,850 acres) some hundreds of miles to the south. Other plantings exceeding 1,000 acres, are in the counties of Monterey (4,100 acres) and San Luis Obispo (1,400 acres).

California (and other US States) Appellations
In some ways, and without conscious effort, the California and Burgundy wine industries are similar; in other respects they are worlds apart. The major companies in both countries sell huge volumes of well-made Chardonnay at affordable prices, given the fluctuations of the US dollar and French franc.

Both California and Burgundy have an appellation embracing the whole state/*département*: California/Bourgogne, meaning that the fruit for those wines may be drawn from anywhere within those geographical boundaries. In the case of the top-shelf wines, Burgundy's best without exception come from small, often very small, to average size single vineyards.

California offers a number of contradictions. The un-oaked Fetzer Sundial Chardonnay, one of America's best known, every-day drinking Chardonnays, produced in six-figure case volume, comes from a *single* vineyard in the northern county of Mendocino. But this single vineyard alone is about one-sixth the size of all Meursault's vineyards combined. Fetzer's top-of-the-line Chardonnays have a California appellation, being blended from fruit drawn from many sources.

Likewise, the burgeoning giant of California Chardonnay, Kendall Jackson in Lake County. Their fruit is sourced from about six different counties over a distance of hundreds of miles, reaching south to Santa Maria. The make-up of their current 'Vintners Reserve' is 28 per cent Santa Barbara county, 29 per cent Monterey county, 4 per cent Napa county, 17 per cent Sonoma county, 10 per cent Lake county and 12 per cent Mendocino county. A fruit salad if ever there was one! But a very successful blend indeed.

Quite the opposite applies at Chateau St Jean (CSJ), where the top of the range Robert Young vineyard Chardonnay has been savoured by royalty (for what that is worth) and is a regular visitor to the White House. This vineyard also exceeds 100 acres. In the very best French tradition, CSJ has consistently produced single vineyard bottlings, unlike its Sonoma counterpart, Simi winery, which goes for the broad brush approach of Sonoma appellation.

The United States, through the Bureau of Alcohol, Tobacco and Firearms, has an approved appellation scheme but its only function is to regulate geographical areas and 'estate bottling' categories. The various classifications are:

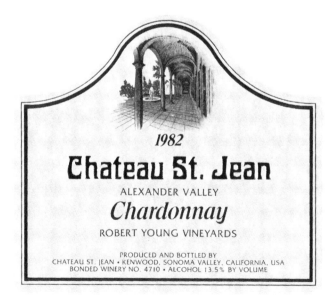

1982

Chateau St. Jean

ALEXANDER VALLEY

Chardonnay

ROBERT YOUNG VINEYARDS

PRODUCED AND BOTTLED BY
CHATEAU ST. JEAN • KENWOOD, SONOMA VALLEY, CALIFORNIA, USA
BONDED WINERY NO. 4710 • ALCOHOL 13.5% BY VOLUME

American Wine is one made from a blend of grapes grown in any number of states;

State i.e. Ohio, Washington, etc, means that the wine is a blend of more than one regional appellation;

County/regional appellation i.e. Santa Barbara county – Finger Lakes region, wine made from a blend of grapes within that geographical area;

Vineyard designation as mentioned in the text, two examples are Robert Young and Sundial;

Estate bottled a wine made from grapes 100 per cent grown, vinified and bottled on the one property.

The New California Philosophies and Styles

'The basic premise is that you need to make the best wine possible; if the best wine is made from a single vineyard you do it. If it's not and you can do it by blending, then so do it, it's as simple as that,' says Richard Arrowood – the winemaker at Chateau St Jean (CSJ) and Arrowood Vineyards.

In response to my question regarding the ever-changing styles of California Chardonnays as opposed to the static styles of Burgundy, Arrowood said, 'Yes, ever-changing is true, we are all searching for a particular style. I wouldn't say it's ever-changing within a particular winery – in some respects our style has been modified, to fit not necessarily consumer perception, although that certainly plays a part, but what we think is best, or better, for the particular wine in question. Do we need to make 14 per cent plus alcohol Chardonnays? No, but we did before because that was important to us. Now we are looking for more finesse, so we're fine-tuning it: I guess that would be the word. We're not drastically changing things, we're not modifying the style of CSJ or Arrowood to fit some bizarre scheme of what I think a fine Chardonnay is. We are trying to make a statement that we can consistently produce Chardonnay of top quality, but it's not always going to taste the same each year because you've got the vagaries of Mother Nature. We now have the tools and facilities to do what we couldn't do many years ago when the weather presented us with a problem.'

How has Arrowood 'fine-tuned' his wines? 'In a phrase, doing less of most things.' In fact, these answers apply to almost all major California Chardonnay producers. Sulphur dioxide is no longer added at the crusher; instead it is added to the juice after crushing. As I mention in Part IV, the timing of sulphur dioxide addition is central to many winemakers' philosophies, and I, for one, believe that the timing of the addition is an important factor in Chardonnay flavour. CSJ, like so many other New World wineries, have reduced their skin contact times considerably, from as much as forty-eight hours to twelve hours maximum.

But the term 'fine-tuning', whether it be an orchestra, car or wine, simply means attending to every minute detail – the difference between a top performance and a very ordinary one. In winemaking, this means a careful study of every facet. For $5 you get a $5 bottle wine. Sadly, in many cases, you also get a $5 bottle for $15 although the wine should be appreciably better. Three times better? I don't think so, even if I understand where the extra money is involved.

Without anticipating word for word what I say about winemaking later in the book, it is important that I go over the main flavour influencing factors and the current state-of-the-art in California; this means the New World in general. The reader may benefit from continual reference to Part Four which I am sure will give her/him a solid understanding of Chardonnay flavours, their derivation and the countless ways that the winemaker can, and does, manipulate wine flavour, structure and texture.

It is a historical fact that people talk about one set of standards and practise another. The wine industry has always known and stated that winemaking starts in the vineyard, although in the New World there has often been a rather half-hearted commitment to the philosophy. I believe that, universally, winemakers are paying greater attention to such finite details as clones, climates, trellising, canopy management, and more specifically, fruit maturity. There also appears to be a gentle hauling back of the desired sugar levels.

The cardinal *perceived* need in today's wines is the media-initiated requirement for wines that last longer, wines that will still be at their 'peak' in fifteen years' time. In view of the fact that 80 per cent of all wine sold is consumed within a week of purchase, why the need for wines that will last ten to twenty years or more? The original California style, and still the most popular by a million miles, is the method of fermenting ripe fruit in stainless steel tanks, cleaning up the wine and giving it some time in oak barrels. This technique makes fresh, fruity, up-front wines to be enjoyed immediately. Maybe some fractions of 'sur-lies' style will be added for complexity; and as a general rule only, anything in the medium-priced range will have an increasing amount of 'sur-lies' wine added. Above $20, most of the wine will be made by the 'sur-lies' method.

'Bâtonnage', the stirring of a wine while on its fermentation lees, has become a central focus in fine-tuning. As more 'sur-lies' fractions are added to the base wine, there is an increase in mouth-feel, complexity, and longevity prospects. Also there is the need to cellar the wine proportionately longer for full enjoyment. This introduces the need to re-educate the consumer, whose first love affair with Chardonnay was for a wine packed with over-ripe fruit, high alcohol and enough burnt oak for a barbecue.

The selection of fermentation yeasts is playing a leading role as we learn more about their flavours, vices and habits. Some wine-makers are using as many as ten different yeasts in selected wine batches to complement the different fruit. The result, when blended, can be a wine with a broad flavour spectrum. Just as the 'warm' area winemaker can obtain the lemony-citrus flavours so familiar to cool climate fruit by adjusting pH with citric acid, so the cool climate winemaker can introduce the warm area tropical fruit flavours by the use of selected yeasts.

In California Chardonnays of the last decade, described as powerful, big and fat, the style almost demanded that all wines undergo malolactic fermentation (MLF). This view has been con-siderably overhauled, with some fruit not going through the process at all, while other fruit is still given 100 per cent MLF. There is certainly a lot of work and experimentation still going on in this area. So we have a situation where there is no MLF at one end of the spectrum and various degrees from 20 per cent MLF through to 100 per cent at the other. Each winemaker can make a case for his current philosophy.

In all, California is undergoing a search for its Chardonnay identity. There is very little, if anything, to fault about the current crop of wines – the winemakers just think that they can do it better; and almost everyone is trying damned hard.

The Napa Valley

While the Sonoma Valley is greater in terms of size and planted vines, and possibly holds pride of place for Chardonnay, the home of California winemaking, and the place with the international reputation, particularly for Cabernet Sauvignon is the Napa Valley. Everybody has, and is entitled to, her/his own opinion on these matters. It would be fair to say that Chardonnay in the New World gained its original impetus from the Napa Valley. Things started to move a mere thirty years ago with the legendary 1957 Hanzell Chardonnay from Sonoma, which first introduced a smack of new French oak to give complexity to what were already basically good wines.

It is interesting that the original gang of big league Napa Char-donnay makers from the 1950s and 1960s, like Beaulieu, Inglenook, Joe Heitz, Charles Krug, Château Montelena and Freemark Abbey have nearly all, to some extent, been overtaken in the fashion stakes by the 'new boys on the block'. However, the small bou-tiques of early days, which included Hanzell, Chalone (no longer a boutique nor in Napa), Mayacamas, Stony Hill and a few others, have maintained their legion of faithful followers even though most still do not provide tasting facilities for the enthusiast, yours truly included.

There is some dispute whether Napa, named after the Napa Woppa Indians, means *home* or *plenty*. It matters little, as either is applicable to this large band of innovative and enthusiastic vine-makers. More than 100 years ago my boyhood hero, Robert Louis Stevenson, summed them up rather well in 'Silverado Squatters'. 'One corner of land after another is tried with one kind of grape after another,' wrote Stevenson. 'This is a failure, that is better, a third best. So, bit by bit, they grope about for their Clos Vougeot and Lafite . . . and the wine is bottled poetry.' They haven't changed one iota in a century!

The Napa Valley, about thirty-five miles long starting at the now famous Los Carneros region on the northern end of San Pablo Bay, terminates somewhere around the hot-springs (and mud-baths) of Calistoga. The valley, ranging from one to five miles wide, is the wine tourists' mecca, due not only to its international fame and top-class wines, but also to the fact that Highway 29 runs along the valley floor. The winery tasting/sales rooms are situated like beads on a string, presenting one of the wine lovers greatest challenges: My advice is visit only three wineries per day.

Carneros is Spanish for sheep, but wine language for Char-donnay and Pinot Noir. It is so cool that only in very hot years will the late ripening Cabernets reach maturity in this single appell-ation straddling both Napa and Sonoma counties. Los Carneros is a viticultural phenomenon in that it is the coolest *and* the most southerly part of the Napa. As you go north through the Valley, as a rule, the climate becomes warmer rather than colder. The San Pablo Bay influence is significant for several viticultural reasons. The winds coming off the Bay help dry off any moisture or rain, the catalysts for bunch rot, and the weather stays warmer during winter and cooler in summer providing ripe fruit with high acids and lower sugar levels – or wines with less alcohol, a major contributor to wine structure and viscosity.

When the original application was made for the Napa Valley

appellation, both growers and winemakers associations agreed that the geographical boundaries would be the 'watershed' of the Valley. This is different from the Napa County boundaries and excluded the Pope, Wooden and Gordon Valleys, whose growers had supplied grapes to valley vinegrowers for years. The Napa name on a bottle of wine is worth a considerable amount to a grape-grower and they were not very keen on the idea of being left out in the cold. The Valley erupted into a slanging match before the Bureau came out in favour of the county political boundaries.

Besides Los Carneros and Napa Valley, one other recognized appellation exists in the Valley: the hilly Howell Mountain area east of St Helena township. The Pope and Chiles Valleys are distinctive regions within the Napa appellation.

One wonders what the good Colonel Yount, who brought the first vines (possibly not Chardonnay) to Napa and planted them just north of the village that now bears his name would think if he could see the Valley's 30,000-odd acres of lush vines and taste the world-class wines that it produces.

A sample of leading Napa Chardonnay producers are:

CARNEROS: Acacia, Bouchaine, Saintsbury

NAPA: Mayacamas, Quail Ridge, Trefethen, Chât. Potelle, Groth, Cartlidge and Brown

YOUNTVILLE: S. Anderson, Monticello

OAKVILLE: Robert Mondavi, Far Niente, Sequoia Grove

RUTHERFORD: Grgich Hills, Rutherford Hills, Cakebread, Inglenook, J. Phelps, Z. D., Beaulieu

ST HELENA: Beringer, Freemark Abbey, Chas Shaw, Martini, Franciscan, Round Hill, Flora Springs, Chappellet, Long Vineyards, Stoney Hill, St Clement, Newton

CALISTOGA: Cuvaison, Chât. Montelena, Sterling

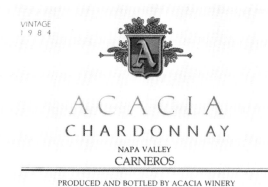

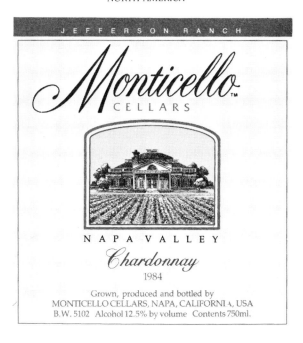

Sonoma County

In its history, California has been an Indian homeland, a Spanish province, a part of Mexico and a Russian outpost. It became a Republic with the raising of the Bear Flag in 1846 and a State of the Union in 1850. Much of this action took place in Sonoma County.

Give or take a few, today Sonoma County has something like 100 wineries; nobody ever quite knows! An amazing feat since it was only *circa* 1812 that the Russians planted the first vines with cuttings believed to have come from the Black Sea area.

A word of warning. Without really trying, Sonoma confuses the visitor with its name being duplicated through the county, valley and town. Within Sonoma County there are at least fourteen identifiably different climatic winegrowing areas and ten appellations or approved viticultural regions, each with an individual part to play in the growing of grapes. There are as many, or more, different soil types and profiles to match the climatic vagaries. The climatic variances are so diverse and so dependent on fogs rolling in from the Pacific Ocean that the UC Co-operative Extension officer in Sonoma County, Richard Sissons, devised his own classifications – 'coastal cool' being those regions cooled by fog, and 'coastal warm' being the areas further inland without fog effects. This climatic phenomenon applies right along the California coast nearly as far south as Los Angeles, where fog becomes smog! The effect of the frequent fog days during summer is to shade the vines and provide cooler ripening conditions which, in many ways, dictates the grape varieties that can be planted.

Almost from the most northern to the most southern extremes, the California coast is guarded by a long series of mountain ranges dotted with irregular openings, commonly called valleys, through which the ocean fogs enter the hinterland. While the coast has a bearing from north-west to south-east, these fog-entry valleys tend to be in a direct south to north direction.

Sonoma County has several towns with a number of wineries within the townsite; Healdsburg is a classic example. This is a marvellous convenience for the winemakers who draw fruit from the three valleys radiating out from the town. By international standards Simi is the most important. Many would say that Clos du Bois with its range of four Chardonnays could contest any Simi claim. William Wheeler winery makes up an interesting trio within a few blocks. In the Windsor area are Landmark, Sonoma Vineyards and Sonoma-Piper, plus the dedicated Chardonnay-only makers, Sonoma Cutrer Vineyards, a wonderful place where you can stop off for a game of croquet!

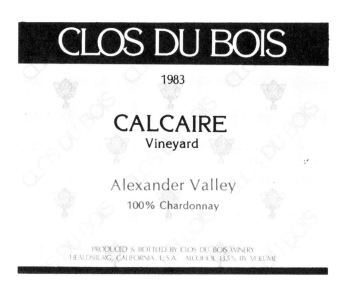

CLOS DU BOIS

1983

CALCAIRE
Vineyard

Alexander Valley
100% Chardonnay

PRODUCED & BOTTLED BY CLOS DU BOIS WINERY
HEALDSBURG, CALIFORNIA, U.S.A.   ALCOHOL 13.5% BY VOLUME

Russian River Valley

Running in a westerly direction from Santa Rosa, or more correctly Windsor on the Interstate Highway 101, right out to the coast at Jenner-by-the-Sea, is the renowned, winding, Russian River Valley, the very heart of Chardonnay in northern California. For promotional purposes, the local winemakers like to refer to the general area as the Russian River Wine Road which takes in the towns of Healdsburg, Geyserville and almost Cloverdale, north along the 101. One might easily consider these wineries north and east of Healdsburg as being in the Alexander Valley. Healdsburg can be seen as the pivotal point for three valleys – Russian River to the west, Dry Creek heading in a north-westerly direction and Alexander Valley away to the northeast.

As a rough, very rough, rule of thumb, the coastal cool regions are ideal for the early-ripening varieties such as Chardonnay and Pinot Noir. The later-season varieties like Sauvignon (blanc), Zinfandel and the Cabernets thrive in the coastal warm regions. In many years these varieties may not ripen in the cooler regions. In fact, Chardonnay and Pinot fruit from Green Valley is much sought after for *méthode champenoise* material as the coolness there slows down full ripening of these early varieties.

Grapes grown in the colder regions can normally command higher prices, both as fruit and as finished wine. In addition to being host to half of the State's Chardonnay acreage planted since 1980, the Russian River Valley has had its average yield lifted by something like 50 per cent, from just over two tons to more than three tonnes per acre, owing to improved clones and viticultural practice. When these came into being during the mid-1980s, California would have had a glut of wine if a lot of fruit had not been used for basic, own-label wines thus creating a new market in the $3–5 price range. As Chardonnay consumption increases and the slowing down in plantings brings a more balanced picture, cool climate fruit will continue to attract premium prices for what are considered the classic labels. Many of these labels belong to the Russian River vignerons who now grow the noble Chardonnay on the plains and low hills of the valley that once provided hops for the San Francisco breweries. While there is, in fact, a hop kiln Winery near Healdsburg, a number of the fascinating hop kiln buildings can still be seen among the vineyards of the valley. Taste has changed.

Leading Chardonnay producers in the Forestville-Guerneville area are: Davis Bynum, De Loach, Dehlinger, Domaine Laurier, Mark West, Iron Horse, Topolos, Jos. Swann.

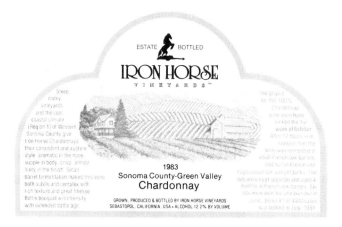

Dry Creek and Alexander Valleys
Dry Creek runs away to the northwest from Healdsburg; Alexander Valley heads off to the north and east. Both are fruit sources for Sonoma.

At the northern end of the Russian River Wine Road above Healdsburg can be found the vineyards and wineries of Dry Creek which include Robert Stemmler and Dry Creek Vineyards, the Alexander Valley home to Estancia, Sausal and Johnson's, while in the Geyserville area there are Trentadue, Souverain, Pedroncelli and Geyser Peak.

Sonoma Valley
The dominating Russian River and its tributaries empty into the Pacific Ocean, the western boundary of Sonoma County. The waters of the Sonoma Valley enter San Francisco Bay, to the south of the county, and this is what makes the Valley – which has wineries on the northern edge of Sonoma township, while the bulk are away to the west – different. This is Jack London country; it is also the home of Buena Vista, one of the State's oldest wineries and abode of Agoston Haraszthy, affectionately known as the father of California wine.

Even though the Valley has but twenty-four, mostly small wineries, on the basis of reputation at least, Sonoma Valley is possibly the centre of California Chardonnay. Glen Ellen and Chateau St Jean are big players in the Chardonnay field, albeit in different segments of the market, with CSJ firmly placed at the top end. And in the fashionable stakes, both Hanzell and Matanzas Creek are very much leaders.

But there are other fine producers in this beautiful valley. Names that quickly come to mind are Adler Fels, Gundlach Bundschu, Kenwood, Kistler, Richardson and St Francis. Only about half have anything in the way of tasting facilities and, as with so many other regions, it is wise to write or telephone ahead if planning a visit. Here, in a distance of only 15–20 miles, one can find the artist's full palette of Chardonnay flavours, ranging from almost pure Burgundian to classic California, or even the $5 Chardonnay. Maybe this is to be expected when the owners either come from, or are based in, places as far away as Hungary, Tokyo, London and Rome!

Mendocino County

As the wine tourist motors along the major roadways of Mendocino County, there is little doubt that this is wine country. On Interstate Highway 101, from just north of the Sonoma County border all the way up to Redwood Valley north of Ukiah, vineyards line both sides of the road, and on Highway 128, the best route to the north California coast, the vineyards of the Anderson Valley can be seen among the hills and forests. This was the area that supplied much of the redwood and fir for housing during the great California goldrush.

The diversity of geography and rainfall makes the Mendocino vineyards appealing, both for the tourist and wine lover. Near the coast, aided by cool nights, the grapes ripen slowly, but grapes do come from everywhere to make the California appellation wines as well as Anderson Valley, Redwood Valley and Mendocino appellations. It is a fascinating place, and the wines represent excellent value for money. Fetzer is the major player, ably supported by Parducci, Weibel, McDowell and Cresta Blanca. In the Anderson Valley is located the USA's most westerly winery and other good Chardonnay producers, such as Navarro, Husch, Handley and Lazy Creek.

Adjoining Mendocino on the east side is Lake County, anything but a major force in terms of population, towns or vineyard acreage. Nonetheless, it is home to Kendall Jackson, a big force in the Chardonnay game. All the Chardonnay grown in Lake County makes about 15,000 cases of wine – Kendall Jackson alone makes 85,000 cases of Chardonnay annually. As mentioned earlier, fruit for this wine comes from six different counties.

Even though Lakeport, the county HQ, has an elevation of nearly 1400 feet, with over 3000 day degrees it is quite a lot warmer than Mendocino (still, that can easily be overcome by a swim in the nearby Clear Lake State park). Two other wineries of Chardonnay significance are Guenoc, about five miles southeast of Middletown, and the co-operative Konocti winery about a mile north of Kelseyville. I would be failing in my duty if I did not advise the reader to visit the wineries of California's two most northern counties.

Livermore Valley

San Francisco, by general agreement, is the dividing line between northern and southern California wine areas. And then there is the 'Bay area', those regions around the expansive San Francisco Bay. Highways 17 and 580 will speed the wine lover to one of them, the Livermore Valley, perhaps the original source of most Californian Chardonnay.

Back in 1912, while a student at UC Davis, Ernest Wente became interested in Chardonnay and looked far and wide for reliable cuttings. He chose one lot from Montpellier, France, and another from the famous Gier Vineyard at nearby Pleasanton. (Chardonnay wines of the Giersburger label had won gold medals in Paris and numerous American expositions.) Over the years Ernest Wente continued to select from these, constantly upgrading each new planting and thus establishing a name for the finest Chardonnays in California.

As late as 1960 records show only 230 acres of Chardonnay in the State, and the Wente plantings had grown to 70 acres at that time. From the 1940s to the 1960s, winegrowers throughout California, including Louis Martini and Fred McCrea of Stony Hill, selected cuttings from this vineyard.

Subsequently, as UC Davis began their clonal selection and propagation programme, now known as the Foundation Plant Material Service (FPMS), the goal was to select clones from the most outstanding commercial vineyards of their type in California. As the Martini Chardonnay vineyard was the most recent selection of the Wente clonal development, Ernest recommended that Drs Harold Olmo and Curtis Alley obtain their cuttings for the University nursery from the Martini vineyard. This is the origin of clone #4, the 'Wente' clone. The Livermore vineyards still contain fifty acres of the original 'Wente' selections dating back to the 1950s.

Wente's and Concannon wineries have been in operation for more than 100 years, which is quite amazing as not only have they survived the universal scourge of phylloxera, but they have also survived a unique viticultural problem – earthquakes! The earthquake of 1906 destroyed a number of wineries in an area which had 7,000 acres of vines at that time. Prohibition wiped out many others. Man, the developer, brought in his bulldozers at the end of World War II and almost completed the devastation, leaving three wineries and about 1,000 acres of vines. Today there are eight wineries and nearly 2,000 acres of vines but only three are important in the Chardonnay stakes: Wente, Concannon and Elliston. The gravelly loams and low rainfalls make for a distinctive Livermore Chardonnay style, one with a devoted following.

Santa Cruz Mountains

The Santa Cruz mountains wine trail, between San Francisco Bay and the Pacific Ocean, comprises vineyards from portions of three counties – Santa Cruz, Santa Clara and San Mateo. Not, strictly speaking, in either northern or southern California, this region forms part of what is known as the Central Coast. It is a stunning, quiet, mountain area of narrow, winding back roads and superb wines. I have wonderful memories of several visits there, of the great reds of Ridge, the whites of Congress Springs, and of wineries which have settings with few equals.

Yet it is fair to say that the region is not geared for tourists, the average operation among the twenty-three wineries is very small. In fact, a number are run as second jobs. Visits to most wineries are by appointment only. None of this detracts from the quality or friendliness; both are in the front rank and the Chardonnay styles range from the north to south poles. Many wines are made from estate-grown fruit, others buy fruit elsewhere and Congress Springs, one of the most successful Chardonnay makers, obtains grapes from specialist growers some distance south near Hollister. The equally notable producer Mt Eden Vineyards is a totally estate-bottled operation. Other producers of commercial quantities and above average quality are David Bruce, Felton Empire, Roudin-Smith, Thomas Fogarty, Santa Cruz and Cronin Vineyards.

Monterey

Internationally, Monterey is probably best known for its most famous son, writer John Steinbeck, whose memory alone draws enormous numbers of people to an already busy tourist centre. Cannery Row, nowadays, is a vital place of interesting stores, restaurants, and fish. Another writer to lift the Monterey image was Richard Henry Dana in his famous novel *Two Years Before the Mast*. In the USA, Monterey is also rather famous for its superb golf courses and tourist facilities. Not far away are two entirely different visitor attractions, Dirty Harry's Carmel (I wonder if the town will ever be able to shrug that off?), and the striking coastline south of Big Sur.

The region is one of the few in California without a vinous background, brought about by two fundamental problems – low rainfall of 8–10 inches annually and strong winds that go through the Valley almost every afternoon like an express train. In the early 1960s, winemakers from neighbouring regions faced by the developers' bulldozers found a solution to the problems: the Salinas River, flowing beneath the well-drained soils, provided ample water for overhead sprinklers and drip-irrigation systems, and the vines could be planted parallel to the prevailing wind.

Twenty years later, Monterey has 35,000 acres of vines, including 4,100 acres of Chardonnay, making it California's third largest Chardonnay producing county. But, just as winemakers came to plant vines in the 100-mile long valley that, in places, is 20 miles wide, so now they take the fruit away to all parts of California. So much so that Monterey fruit could become a major component of any California style, regardless of where it is made. Some of the biggest companies in the State, Almaden, Paul Masson, Mirassou and Wente Bros have their processing facilities in adjoining counties. Mirassou crushes the fruit on the spot and takes only the juice to San Jose.

Despite this, Monterey County is still home to several of the State's most outstanding Chardonnay producers notably Chalone, Jekyl, J. Lohr, Morgan and Ventana, while Monterey Cellars continually rate tops in the commercial Chardonnay category. Yet, again, few offer anything to the visitor without prior arrangements. The wine lover must be well organized in advance.

South Central Coast

While most southern parts of California produce Chardonnay of some considerable merit, the real action is centred in the counties of San Luis Obispo and Santa Barbara. Both have two distinct regions.

San Luis Obispo County contains the regions of Paso Robles and Edna Valley, while Santa Barbara has the established region of Santa Ynez and the burgeoning area of Santa Maria.

Although about a thirty-minute drive inland from the Pacific

Ocean, Paso, Robles, mid-way between San Francisco and Los Angeles on Interstate Highway 101 at the northern end of San Luis Obispo County, is still considered part of the Central Coast wine region. Like so much of the California coastal regions, north and south, the Coast Ranges which run into the Los Padres National park and eventually become the Sierra Madre Mountains, provide vineyard sites in valleys and hills. Paso Robles vineyards vary in altitude from 600–1,900 feet on their mainly alluvial sandy loam soils.

The 1,500 acres of Chardonnay vines have a number of owners and makers, mainly between the towns of San Miguel and Temple-ton. Some date back 100 years but most have been developed in the last decade. Once again, it's wise to plan and telephone ahead. The prominent Chardonnay producers are Adelia Cellars, Belli and Sauret, Castoro, Creston Manor, Eberle, Estrella River, Martin Bros, Mastantuono and Wild Horse – yes, this is rodeo country!

Non-Americans might find the repeated California duplication of town/winery, city/county names a little confusing. About twenty-seven miles south of Paso Robles is the city of San Luis Obispo and another five miles southwest is the Edna Valley wine region, which has a very distinguished Edna Valley Chardonnay winery. The region is small, the reputation big. Also in the Chardonnay game is the large Corbett Canyon Winery and the not so large Chamisal.

Down Highway 101 through Arroya Grande, the long-nosed wine lover will come to Santa Maria, a name on the lips of almost every California Chardonnay aficionado. This is the source of so much good fruit and the reader may recall that some went as far north as Lake County, around 400 miles. During 1987 there was quite a financial battle for control of the well-established Tepesquet vineyard, with portions going to the Mondavi and Kendall-Jackson interests. This is the case with lots of Santa Maria fruit, conditions are so ideal that away it goes to distant wineries.

Santa Ynez Valley was a relatively new area in the 1970s but is now recognized all over the country as one of the finest for the Burgundy varieties Pinot Noir and Chardonnay. However, they are a tight-knit group who do not give away a gram of information. Nobody, but nobody, wanted to provide any information, and had it not been for previous visits the area would have been left out.

Sanford and Benedict, Brander, Firestone, Zaca Mesa, Santa Ynez and Au Bon Climat are all leading producers of Chardonnay in an area well known for pea soup and the Danish look-alike village of Solvang, one of California's premium tourist attractions.

Other California Regions

In the San Joaquin Valley region of Fresno-Madera can be found California State University (where so many winemakers have learnt their craft) and California's largest grape-growing region. With a heat summation (for explanation, see page 139) of around 4000°F and only 8–14 inches of natural rainfall, the region, like much of the Australian and Spanish inland vineyards, is dependent on vast irrigation schemes. These are hostile environments for vines, but with continued clonal selection, marriage of rootstocks and good vineyard management, these regions do produce worthy wines.

About sixty acres of Chardonnay grow here on what is known as Hanford loam and other light sandy loam soils. The principal producer is Papagni Vineyards.

Chardonnay is grown and made in several areas to the south and west of Los Angeles, which is generally regarded as the birthplace of the California wine industry. Not only was LA the start of the Franciscan Fathers chain of vineyards but also the area close to Disneyland at Anaheim was, a century ago, a German settlement and California's largest vineyard.

Within a pleasant day's drive from Los Angeles one can reach either the eastern wine areas around Cucamonga and San Bernardino County, or head south along Highway 15 to Temecula and Escondido. In the east there are two good Chardonnay producers – Filsinger and Hart wineries.

The Pacific Northwest

The Pacific Northwest is not a well-known geographical region outside North America. This vast area includes the states of Oregon and Washington in the USA, and British Columbia in Canada. For our purposes it will also include the state of Idaho, where viticulture is proceeding apace in a land better known for its potatoes than its Pinots.

Not only is the Pacific Northwest an exciting new winegrowing frontier, but its scenery is equal to anything, anywhere in the world; quite breathtaking in all four areas.

Washington State is by far the largest producer in this area and, outside California, the state with the largest plantings of *vinifera* varieties in the USA. New York State has more grapes, but the

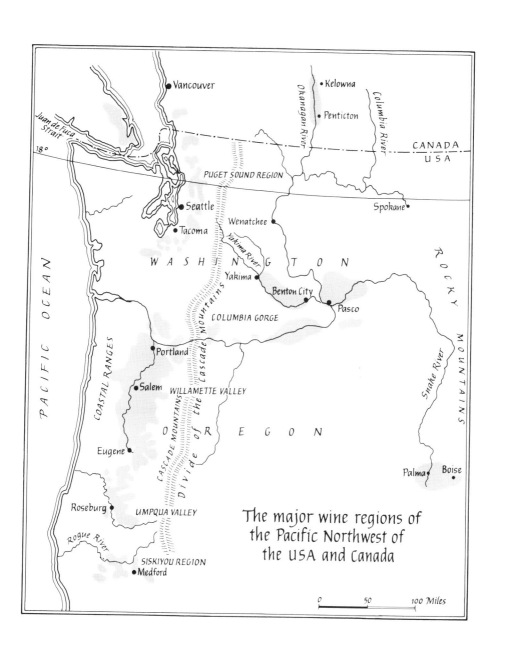

The major wine regions of
the Pacific Northwest of
the USA and Canada

0   50   100 Miles

largest proportion is of non-*vinifera* varieties used for grape juice, jellies and jams.

Washington State

Most vineyards are planted east of the Cascade Mountains in the volcanic soils of the Columbia Valley, centred on Yakima at the junction of Highways I-82 and 12, and Walla Walla 130 miles to the southeast almost on the Oregon border. Other popular areas are Spokane, and west of Seattle there are several cool climate specialists.

Washington has two major corporate wineries with national distribution, and several shareholder operations, but the greater number of wineries are small family partnerships – just like the wine industry world-wide.

Washington has fifty-five Chardonnay vineyards, the largest being 212 acres and the smallest one acre, which are planted on a variety of loam, sandy loam soils. The clones are predominantly the Davis selections and are planted on their own roots. Rootstocks, as yet, have not been found useful.

For unknown reasons, Washington has a penchant for things French. This seems to be a part of the US Pacific Northwest, something of a 'cultural cringe', which the region should be overcoming after a couple of decades of doing their own thing and realizing that techniques, temperatures, micro-climates and every other facet of winegrowing are not transportable from one vineyard to another, let alone across oceans or cultures. To the best of my knowledge, the wines of the region can stand on their own two feet and need not worry about imitating California, Chablis or Coonawarra.

Oregon

If it had not been for their involvement in, and promotion of, the elusive Pinot Noir variety, I doubt that many people would have heard of Oregon as a wine-producing state. Even though, as of 1988, there are only about 420 hectares of Pinot Noir planted in the State, and, according to leading Willamette Valley producer, David Adelsheim, its recognition is out of all proportion to its size. It is a fact that where Pinot Noir can grow and flourish, so can Chardonnay, and it is flourishing in Oregon, all 350 hectares of it.

Bill Sokol, one of the brighter stars of the more southern Umpqua Valley, has a lot of faith in the future of Chardonnay in each of Oregon's four major producing regions – the Columbia, Willamette, Rogue and Umpqua Valleys.

While the inter-mountain location of both Willamette and Umpqua Valleys give them a similar climate, the increased warmth of Umpqua, as a general rule, makes for a different and bigger style of Chardonnay. The more southerly Rogue Valley, west of the Cascade Mountains, also enjoys warmer summers providing the necessary natural elements for different wine styles, thus ensuring that Oregon is a place of considerable interest for the Chardonnay lover.

At the time of writing, Oregon had 187 vineyards, located in 16 counties, of which about 150 had plantings of Chardonnay; the largest planting is 30 hectares and the smallest 1 hectare. Most, if not all, vines are self-rooted. Something like 140 of the State's total vineyards are less than 8 hectares and the average yield of Chardonnay is in the order of 6.5 tonnes per hectare. What all this means is that the Oregon industry is a low volume producer of good to high quality wine, necessarily aimed at the upper end of the market.

If any one thing is holding back the rapid development of Chardonnay in Oregon it is the lack of new clones. UCD 5 (#108) is the standard clone and has done little to enthuse Oregon growers. They await official clearance for more suitable European clones, predicted for 1988, but it will be well into the 1990s before they have any answers about their suitability.

Maybe this is fortuitous, as the history of Oregon Chardonnay making has been a chequered one. The present-day winemakers must look over their shoulders with a wry smile at techniques used during the last two decades. There can be no doubt that today's skills have been fine-tuned to the stage that most makers can produce a very good bottle of wine. Yet they are the first to acknowledge that the learning curve is a long one. As David Adelsheim says, the improvements will be incremental rather than dramatic; they certainly are a keen and determined lot. Put Oregon down as one of the places to watch over the next decade.

Leading producers of Chardonnay in Oregon would include Adelsheim, Amity, Cameron, Eyrie, Forgeron, Peter Adams, Rex Hill, Sokol Blosser, Valley View, Veritas, Yamhill Valley and Tualatin.

Idaho

On the escarpments above the impressive Snake River a new industry is coming to life among Idaho's potato fields. This is

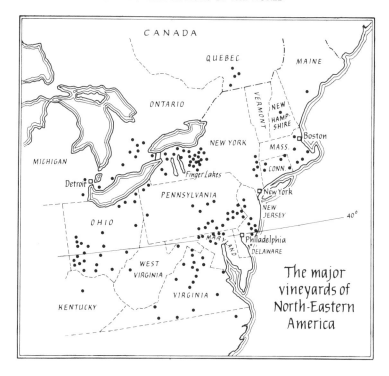

The major vineyards of North-Eastern America

first-class country for growing Chardonnay despite the very strong Mormon teetotal population and cowboy beer-drinkers. Just west of the state capital Boise are a number of excellent vineyards around Caldwell – Valley Vintners, Brundage Cellars and Château Ste Chappelle. The growing of Chardonnay in Idaho is still too fledgling an industry to cite statistics.

North-Eastern America

It is a little known fact that grapegrowing and winemaking in north-eastern USA and eastern Canada has been a regular agricultural pursuit since the earliest explorers arrived on the Atlantic seaboard, commencing in the days when Lief Ericsonn named the area Vinland.

In the last half of the nineteenth century, Ohio, Missouri and New York lead the USA in wine production, and in 1871 the largest winery on the continent was the Golden Eagle winery in Ohio. Wines from east of the Rockies competed directly with those from Europe in the best restaurants and achieved international recognition by winning medal after medal at many of the world expositions held between 1873 and 1900.

During these years, and until World War II, the wine industry in eastern North America concentrated on making champagnes, ports, sherries, and the sweeter wines that could be made from such native varieties as Catawba, Concord, Delaware and Niagara. These varieties, unfortunately, had a major drawback in that they were not suitable for making dry table wines. Nor was there any substitute. Attempts had been made since the early 1600s to grow *vinifera* varieties imported from Europe, but a combination of insects, disease and harsh winters in the east lead to three centuries of failure in growing *vinifera* varieties.

As in so many other places the end of the war marked the beginning of the modern-day wine industry in the northeast. At this time it became possible to grow grapes that would make dry table wines of acceptable quality. The French hybrid grapes were introduced from Europe, and these grapes were both well suited for winemaking and well adapted to the difficult growing conditions. In fact, besides being almost unknown, I believe they are also the world's most under-rated wines. About the same time, herbicides and fungicides were developed to control various diseases, making it possible to grow *vinifera* varieties in the east for the first time.

Slowly interest began to increase in growing these 'new' varieties and in making wine from them. The few wineries in the east at the end of World War II were mainly larger wineries that dated back to the previous century. Gradually, without fanfare, they were joined by small wineries producing only a few thousand gallons of wine a year. The dramatic growth of the wine industry in the east is most evident in the sharp increase of the small 'boutique', or farm, wineries that have sprung up in the last twenty-five years. There are now far more than 400 wineries east of the Rocky Mountains and the number keeps growing. In many areas, the establishment of farm wineries had to wait until the necessary laws were passed by state legislatures. While most states have now passed some form of farm winery law (and 'some form' should be stressed due to the archaic thinking in many places, particularly in those states of the so-called 'Bible-belt' where religion and hypocrisy go hand-in-hand) the political struggle continues to liberalize the often restrictive laws governing the marketing and sale of wine.

Even though giant strides have been made in the east, particularly in relation to growing Chardonnay, more than thirty years ago one of the pioneers, the much-loved Charles Fournier, former President of New York's Gold Seal winery, issued a warning that still should not go unheeded. 'Don't recommend Chardonnay to growers who are going to depend on it as a means of a livelihood selling grapes,' he said, 'but it is part of the enterprise in which growing and winemaking are integrated. It is for the grower who is also the winemaker. Under these circumstances Chardonnay is very attractive. As a grapegrowing enterprise (in the northeast) Chardonnay is not viable, I don't think it is reasonable to look on these cold-tender varieties as being as attractive as our hardy American varieties. The number of Chardonnay crops we can achieve per decade is far less than what we can achieve with the American varieties.'

Although the first Chardonnay was planted at Bright's Wines, Ontario, Canada by dedicated vinegrower George Hostetter, Charles Fournier in conjunction with the incredible Dr K. Franks, were mainly responsible for doing the seemingly impossible – facilitating the growing of *vinifera* in the east. Many devoted people since have made notable contributions to the development of Chardonnay there and I strongly believe that these wines are now right up there with the world's best. But it was Konstantin Frank who had the ultimate vision, the vision that if *vinifera* could survive the depths of the Russian winters, it could survive in the northeast of the American continent. Critics, of which there were many, said he was all sorts of things, an eccentric being the kindest of all, but he never wavered and today there are thousands of acres of *vinifera* growing east of the Rockies as a monument to his stubbornness. Today, New York State has 800 acres of Chardonnay mainly in Finger Lakes and Long Island – and is planted in half of the State's eighty wineries.

New York State

To wine lovers the world over, New York is a place where they can find such famous tourist attractions as Fifth Avenue, Broadway, Times Square, the Statue of Liberty and the Empire State building. These are all part of Manhattan Island, or the city of New York, NY, tucked away in the bottom south-east boundary of a rather large state, also called New York. This end of the State faces the Atlantic Ocean, but you can drive 500 miles in a straight line and still be in New York, this time facing Lake Erie and Canada across the border. New York is a state of diverse climates, geography and people. The Chardonnay lover will be concerned with four wine-producing areas; the Finger Lakes – so named because they look like a hand-print on the map, Chautauqua County – Lake Erie, Long Island and the Hudson River.

The Finger Lakes

The Finger Lakes viticultural region, bounded on the east by Inter-state Highway 81 and on the north by Highway I-90 is the state's main wine centre. The lakes all bear Indian names, and most of the vineyards and wineries are on the slopes of Lakes Keuka, Seneca, and Cayuga, while the largest of the companies, Canandaigua, is alone on the northern end of Lake Canandaigua. Under the Widmer label, this company began making Chardonnay in 1987.

The pioneering *vinifera* work of Konstantin Frank and Charles Fournier took place here in the Finger Lakes, starting at the Geneva research station where Frank was unhappily employed due to the belief that only hybrids would grow in the cold northeast, then Gold Seal, now part of The Taylor Wine Co. at Hammondsport, and finally at Frank's own property, Vinifera Wine Cellars, also high above Hammondsport, at the southern end of Keuka Lake.

At the end of the 1980s, excellent Chardonnays are made at many of the thirty plus wineries around the lakes along with stunning Rieslings and some really exciting hybrid grape varieties, both red and white. In fact, Chardonnay blended with the hybrids such as Seyval Blanc and the American varieties Catawba and Delaware, makes a splendid bottle of bubbly. Wagner's was high-lighted in the London tasting I conducted, and continues to be a major force in US competitions. Taylor's has both still and spark-ling Chardonnays of considerable merit, bearing in mind that until recently they were the only producer capable of sufficient quan-tities to have national distribution. And Glenora is a worthy label and in 1987 became the State's leading Chardonnay producer. Among the boutiques of the Finger Lakes, Bob and Mary Plane invite all-comers to better their Chardonnay, while Hermann Weimer and Bob McGregor also understand what Chardonnay is all about. Heron Hill and Knapp's also show you do not have to travel far in the area to taste a good bottle of wine, and Wickham, Hazlitt 1852 Vineyards, Great Western and Finger Lakes Wine Cellars have also been among the medal winners of late.

Lake Erie

Away to the northwest, some distance along the Interstate 90 from the large, and in winter, snowy city of Buffalo, the

Chardonnay lover will come to the 'Concord-belt' (nothing to do with fast aeroplanes) on the shores of Lake Erie. Here can be found something like 20,000 acres of grape vines, mostly the American variety Concord, which are used for jams, juice and jelly. It was here that the dreaded Prohibition movement started, and a nation lost its way for fifteen years. Obviously, conditions are similar here to the other, Canadian, side of the lake, a place for viticultural heroes. The Woodbury vineyard at Dunkirk, NY, has an enviable reputation for its Chardonnay; sadly it is a long time since I've enjoyed a bottle.

Hudson River

After seeing the sights of Manhattan, the Chardonnay lover can head either east or north for one and a half hours and find many good bottles. The northerly route will proceed along the Hudson River, and once clear of the Manhattan traffic jungle the riverside drive along the Pallisades Parkway to Bear Mountain is a memorable experience with many spectacular viewing points spaced above the river. West Park Vineyards is a specialist Chardonnay operation (they sell nothing else), while some of the juice comes from out-of-state (I find no problem with that). Benmarl Vineyards, with its superb views and host, is a jewel in an area that has been producing wine for more than 200 years. Windsor Vineyards, also at Marlboro, has recently been among the winners at NY contests. No doubt others have started making Chardonnay since my last visit. For example, Brotherhood – America's oldest winery – became one of its newest Chardonnay producers with the 1987 vintage.

Long Island

Leaving Broadway behind and heading eastwards, the wine tourist will aim for Riverhead, New York, between the North and South Forks of Long Island. Here among the fertile soils that once supplied New York with potatoes are the vines of one of the USA's most exciting new wine areas. It is real 'country club' stuff, no place for the $5-a-day brigade. Everything is expensive here: this is the playground of the wealthy Manhattan set. But its island situation means that normally it does not suffer the severe winter weather that makes *vinifera* growing a hazardous occupation in the rest of New York State. As Dr Nelson Shaulis says, 'The advent of *vinifera* growing on Long Island has really opened this up in eastern north America. There [Long Island] the question is not shall we grow *vinifera*, but rather, which *vinifera*? It would be wrong to grow non-*vinifera* there; it's a prime site that is expanding rapidly. They will get their 9–10 crops per decade and 4–6 tons per acre'.

In terms of climate, there is optimism that this part of Long Island will prove to be one of the best areas to grow *vinifera* in the east. There is a 210-day growing season, an amount of sunlight comparable to California's Napa Valley, and mild winters where the temperature rarely falls below 0°F.

As we head for 1990, Long Island has thirty vineyards producing Chardonnay with plantings varying from one to fifty acres which produce about 1,500 US tons annually, a substantial quantity at this time. Not all of this is used on the island, some going to other makers in Connecticut, Pennsylvania, New Jersey and upstate New York. However, prices and demand for Long Island wines will, more than likely, keep much of future production at home. It is probably easier to find a good bottle of Chardonnay on Long Island than anywhere else in the east. Notable among producers, with at least a couple of years track-record, are, in alphabetical order: Bridgehampton, Hargrave, Lenz, Le Reve, Palmer, Pindar and Peconic Bay.

The Golden Triangle

Quite a novel title for the mid-Atlantic states of Pennsylvania, Maryland and Virginia. Although William Penn planted the first vines way back in 1684, the modern wine history of Pennsylvania started (as with similar legislation in most other eastern states), with the passing of the Limited Wineries Act in 1968. The State now has more than forty wineries stretching from near Philadelphia in the south-east corner, to the shores of Lake Erie over 400 miles away. It is fair to say that most of the Chardonnay action is at the Atlantic end of Pennsylvania, and although Chardonnay acreage is limited, the grapegrower is learning to live with the problems associated with a new environment. Around the historic sites of Brandywine and Chadds Ford there are several producers who are finding ready markets for their Chardonnay out-of-state as well as at home in Pennsylvania. Former professional musician Eric Miller, of the Chaddsford Wine Company, learnt the wine craft with his distinguished father, illustrator/author/winemaker Mark Miller, at the Benmarl Winery on the banks of the Hudson River in New York, before finding his own small piece of America with wine author wife, Lee. John Crough at Allegro Vineyards, Brogue, is another Pennsylvania winery running-hot with Chardonnay.

In neighbouring Maryland, the scene is quite a lot smaller, but there are still a couple of outstanding winemakers. I will never forget my first bottle of Catoctin Cabernet from Brookville MD, an outstanding wine. Along with the Byrd Vineyards at Myersville and Elk Run, Catoctin makes up a splendid trio in a state where French hybrids found great strength in the early days of eastern winegrowing.

Further to the south in Virginia is where the third President of the USA, Thomas Jefferson, tried to grow *vinifera* vines for thirty years and finally gave up in 1808. As in Ohio and New York, the state government in Virginia is supportive of the wine industry, and the marketing and promotion efforts are funded far beyond what the growers and makers could do for themselves. This has been a smart move in all three states, as both the wine and tourist industries have enjoyed a marked increase in the number of visitors. As Virginia approaches forty wineries state-wide, a number of very good Chardonnay makers quickly come to mind; Autumn Hill, Dominion, Ingleside, Meredyth, Misty Mountain, Montdomaine, Naked Mountain, Oak Knoll, Oakencroft, Oasis, Piedmont and Plantation.

As part of the viticultural learning curve, much experimentation is taking place in the 'Golden Triangle', as in many other states in the east. Canopy management and manipulation appears to be the central theme. This really means arranging the vine canopy by various trellising types and trimming the leaves so that the vines are opened up. This ensure that sufficient sunshine is able to ripen the fruit to obtain maximum natural sugar levels. Certainly, the 'Golden Triangle' is an historic, scenic and interesting area to visit; I love it – and the people even more so!

Texas

Of all the places in the world that is likely to capture the imagination of the cowboy lover, it is Texas. The Texans work very hard at developing that image. What a lot of people do not know is that Texas works almost, well almost, as hard at making wine – very good wine – and some not so good. While Texans like to think that their state, and everything else about Texas is *big*, the truth is that *three* states the size of Texas can be comfortably fitted into Western Australia, where they also make superb wine! All jokes aside, some very wonderful bottles of Chardonnay have been and continue to be made in the Lone Star state. The perceived view of Texas certainly is not one of high mountain ranges, but up in the 'panhandle', that part of Texas squeezed in between Oklahoma and New Mexico, can be found the most unlikely home of Chardonnay. Centred on the city of Lubbock, a 'dry' city, where the evils of neo-Prohibitionism and the crazy values that go with it have not left. Yet, here (on the High Plains), some 3,000-plus feet above sea level is a thriving grape and wine industry. Oh no, you cannot buy a bottle of wine in town, but drive across the city limits and there is a multi-choice of liquor stores, standing in the middle of nowhere. Not far from such symbols of a sober and demented, church-dictated society, can be found Llano Estacado ('staked plains') winery, an unreal and impossible dream come true. I have presented the wines of Llano Estacado to wine lovers the world over in seminars designed to teach about the joys and healthful beauty of wine – the very stuff that, in more honest religious services, is presented as the blood of Christ. (If you think I'm being hard on these religious parasites, just go to Texas and try and get a drink in many parts of the State, including the city of Dallas. Let me assure you that the real truth is stranger than fiction.)

Also on the High Plains area among the forty vineyards that grow Chardonnay can be found Pheasant Ridge, another maker of fine Chardonnay. Texas has the shortest Chardonnay growing season in the northern hemisphere, brought about by its 4,300 day degrees. Although there is no phylloxera in Texas these days, many of the far-sighted growers are planting Chardonnay on SO4 and 3309 rootstocks. The sandy loams of the High Plains make it a desirable situation for nematodes (a root-sucking pest) which have appeared in some areas.

Several other promising areas for Chardonnay can be found away to the southeast of Lubbock. At Ballinger is the Bluebonnet Hill Winery of Antoine and Danielle Albert with eighteen acres of Chardonnay in their 57-acre vineyards. Just east of State capital Austin is the Messina Hof winery which makes Chardonnay from Lubbock fruit. I also hear good reports about Wimberley Valley at Driftwood, and their Chardonnay.

Out west at Fort Stockton the giant Cortier Estate, formerly St Genevieve, is also ready to launch another Texas Chardonnay on to the market.

Some idea of the Texas wine industry can be gauged by a couple of paragraphs from the Texas Grape Growers' Association newsletter which states:

By the end of 1987, Texas had approximately 4,500 acres of

vinifera wine grapes planted. Of that amount about 2,000 acres are located on the High Plains, 1,300 in the Trans-Pecos, 400 in the Hill Country, 200 in the Cross Timbers and 200 in north Texas with smaller amounts scattered from Bryan to Del Rio.' In another interesting paragraph the president says, 'Another positive measure of the steady growth of our industry is the award-winning wines being produced. In 1987, Texas wines won a similar percentage of medals at the International Intervin competition as did California. Australia won considerably higher percentage than did either California or Texas.

Other USA States

Although in small quantities, Chardonnay is planted in many states, from Idaho to Georgia and from New Mexico to Connecticut. In many ways these plantings represent a major viticultural break-through in adapting the vine to the extremes of climatic conditions – freezing winters to humid summers. What more can one ask of a single-plant species?

The northern winters along the shores of Ohio on Lake Erie are severe. Being shallower than neighbouring Lake Ontario, the vast expanse of Lake Erie regularly freezes over during a normal winter. The proximity of vineyards to the lake is critical in mid-winter as well as during spring frosts.

Although Ohio has a sprinkling of vineyards all over the state, the only two Chardonnay areas are in the northwest on North Bass Island and in the northeast almost on the Pennsylvania border at Conneaut. While I have not experienced the Island wines, I have enjoyed many a good bottle of Markko and the ex-Château Lagniappe Chardonnay, both splendid examples of the 'classic' style. About sixty miles either east or west of Cleveland will bring the wine lover close to the Ohio action. Château Debonne at Madison, en route to Conneaut, is building a good reputation for fine Chardonnay. Interesting soils can be found around the lake: what is called plateau silt loam in the northeast and clay and limestone in the northwest. Most of the vine cuttings are from the New York Dr Frank selection which in the northwest are grafted on to rootstocks 3309 and SO4 while the north-east cuttings have been grafted on to such rootstocks as 1616, 5BB, 26G and others.

These two regions of Ohio are a marvellous example of diverse micro-climates, despite both being on the lake and, if it is important, within the same political jurisdiction. The northeast is 600–900 feet above sea level, has 60 inches of rain annually and a heat summation of about 2,900°F. At Put-In-Bay the weather station for our north-west figures, the recordings there are 550 feet above sea level, 27 inches of rainfall and heat summation of 3,200°F. These figures would make it difficult for the two areas to produce similar wines. Ohio has four Chardonnay vineyards producing about 70 tons of fruit from 25 acres.

Running right through the centre of Long Island Sound is the New York/Connecticut State boundary. We have already seen how the maritime climate influences the ability to grow Chardonnay on Long Island; unfortunately Connecticut vineyards are some distance inland and do not enjoy the same caress of the ocean, rather the chill of the continental climate. This does not stop the brave from soldiering on, however, and Chardonnay does grow, and is produced, in Connecticut. Two excellent examples are Haight Vineyards with some local and some out-of-state fruit, and Crosswinds with local fruit. Both have been rubbing shoulders with the best of the eastern Chardonnays.

Moving down the Atlantic coast to New Jersey where the vine-grower is faced with several problems, not the least being the age-old winter kill problem that is encountered by all growers at the edge of viticultural limits. But there is at least one unique problem – deer. These New Jersey deer wait until a week or ten days prior to harvest then move in and eat the crop. Dan Vernon at Tewkesbury Wine Cellars relates that not only are the deer selective in the varieties they choose, but it not unusual to see a group of about six deer actually munching away at the grapes in the rows ahead of the pickers. A poll taken among the deer of New Jersey has Chardonnay as the number one favourite! This forces New Jersey winemakers to bring fruit in from Pennsylvania and New York. Prominent among the Chardonnay producers in the Garden State are Alba Winery, Tewkesbury at Lebanon and Tomasello Winery at Hammonton.

CANADA

Few people, including most Canadians, are aware of Canada's contribution to the world of wine. It is estimated that less than 20 per cent of Canadians partake of the world's healthiest beverage, despite the nation's 20-plus million gallon production. It has been said that there is no such thing as Canadian wine. This may have been true little more than ten years ago when most wine was made from imported grapes, juice and concentrates from as far afield as Europe and California. While this is still very much a part of Canadian winemaking I am delighted to say that many wonderful bottles of Canadian Chardonnay are now being made from Canadian-grown grapes.

Canadians are probably the worst-served consumers in the English-speaking world; probably because they are only half in the English-speaking world! The distribution of wine is totally strangled by government monopolies in the various provinces to the extent that I often wonder what constitutes democracy in North America. While governments continue to lump together the undisputed health benefits of wine with the evils of hard liquor, an ignorant public will continue to be confused about what is right and what is wrong. The greed of the Canadian provincial governments is highlighted by the fact that the Quebec control board, or Société des Alcools de Québec (SAQ) as it is known locally, is reputedly the world's largest bottler of French wine! Unlike all other provinces where wine is only sold by government stores, Quebec is going through de-regulation, of sorts.

While much space has been given earlier in this book to the futility of comparative international judgements (on wine), free enterprise is either unrestricted or it is not allowed at all. I have always wondered what the churchgoing do-gooders, who dominate the thinking and actions of legislators, would think if they were told where and when they could worship in the same way as wine drinkers are legislated against. It is high time the world at large took the trouble carefully to consider the difference between wine, as a beverage with meals, and hard liquor. And while we have government owned and regulated stores such as in Canada and twenty or more US states, wine will only ever be viewed as a revenue producer, the same as motor vehicle licences or traffic fines.

In Québec and British Columbia, local wines are marked up something in excess of 40 per cent while imported wines are socked with more than 100 per cent. In the non-producing provinces, both Canadian and imported wines are treated with the same savage taxes. Free trade with the USA and a recent GATT ruling which condemns Canadian liquor policy should eliminate these differential mark ups. I hope so. No one deserves the shabby treatment handed out to Canadian wine lovers and producers.

Western Canada

About five hours' drive to the east and southeast of Vancouver are the areas which represent a vital and exciting part of the overall progression of fine wine in the northwest. While the Okanagan Valley is the focus of development in western Canada, other areas such as the Similkameen Valley and, to a lesser extent, Vancouver Island, are playing their part in British Columbia.

Being on the same latitude as Champagne and the German Rhine Valley, the vineyards of British Columbia have attracted a lot of interest from Europe, particularly from Germany, in the development of grapegrowing and winemaking. This German influence has seen the internationally unfashionable Riesling emerge as the number one wine style. Canadian friends tell me that Riesling is easier to sell than Chardonnay because of its fruity flavour and consumer acceptance. In a country where 'weirdo' wine names are legendary (try Spumante Bambino, Fuddle Duck, Alpenweiss or Similkameen Superior), British Columbia has two Rieslings – the standard German Riesling which is known locally as Johannisberg Riesling and the top-planted Okanagan Riesling, a cold-hardy variety from Hungary.

Nonetheless, a very dedicated team of commercial viticulturists and Summerland research station scientists, are making the most of British Columbia's more favourable climate for other *vinifera* varieties. Quite amazing work has been done with the production of an atlas, based on climate and soil characteristics, which will help identify suitable viticultural sites in both the Okanagan and Similkameen Valleys.

The government of British Columbia has, in many ways, been supportive of the grape and wine industry and is the only one which makes a determined effort to discriminate between wine and hard liquor. There is enormous pride and zeal about the local wine industry, and I, for one, will be watching very closely the future of Chardonnay in British Columbia. Reliable producers are Bright's, Divino, Mission Hill and Sumac Ridge.

Eastern Canada

I n eastern Canada there are three wine-producing areas, two in the province of Ontario and one in Nova Scotia. Both Ontario's regions are on peninsular-like strips of land bordering Lake Erie. The Niagara Peninsula, with Lake Ontario on the north side and Lake Erie on the south, has far and away the largest plantings in Canada and is also the main centre for Chardonnay.

Bright's Wines Ltd, Canada's largest and oldest wine company, had the good fortune to benefit from the services of viticulturist, George W. B. Hostetter who brought many innovations to Canadian viticulture, including Chardonnay. In fact, Bright's has been making Chardonnay since 1956, long before most of the other famous names in the northeast. Bright's also showed enormous wisdom in backing Hostetter's pioneering work and this has kept the company ahead of the game. Both Bright's and Hostetter have been generous in making any information freely available to aspiring viticulturists on both sides of the Canadian border. New York State and Canadian viticulturists share similar problems and solutions. Just as the Geneva NY research station has made major breakthroughs in cold climate viticulture, so the Vineland station in Ontario has made an equally impressive contribution.

Ontario

Although Chardonnay is one of the more winter-hardy varieties, it is tested to the limit in Ontario where winter temperatures can plummet to minus 25°C, the sort of temperatures disliked by *vinifera* cultivars other than Chardonnay and Riesling. Canada can have moderately warm winters which will fool Chardonnay into prematurely beginning sap movement for the start of another annual cycle. Should temperatures suddenly drop, the tender little buds will be destroyed and the best a vinegrower can hope for is a second budding which might provide a minimum crop.

So that the reader can understand the severity of winter in this part of the world, let Canadian scientist Dr Helen Fisher explain a unique feature of viticulture in north-eastern America – the multiple trunk system of vinegrowing:

> Most varieties that are subject to winter injury are grown with at least two and sometimes up to four trunks per vine. This complicates pruning and training and the grower must be very careful not to over-crop the vine by leaving too many canes per trunk. The reasoning behind this messy pruning system is insurance. If we have a cold winter (i.e. $-20°$ to $-25°$ C), the trunk of a vine may be injured. There appears to be a difference in cold susceptibility depending on age. Therefore, the multiple trunks are not of the same age. This allows for a differential in the degree of injury as well as a probability of always having a portion of the vine capable of cropping or at least of unimpeded growth. This also means a vine can be successfully renewed without losing total cropping. With a succession of mild, but still injurious weather, there is an accumulation of injury that must be addressed by renewal in time. Multiple trunks also allow for this possibility.

With only about 170 growing days for Chardonnay in Ontario, acids are high, pH levels low, and sugar levels reach a similar level to Chablis. Chaptalization is legal in Canada and is often used to make a more balanced wine, with, say, two per cent sugar added. Rootstock trials at the Vineland Horticultural Research Station show good results with California clones on rootstocks 3309 and 4453 producing sugar levels about 18–19° brix, and about 20° brix in good years.

Latest figures available for Ontario show Chardonnay plantings at 400 acres. As with other northern continents where the north-east is subject to coldness, high rainfall and humidity, in bad climatic years the variety suffers somewhat from grey rot (*botrytis*) in eastern Canada.

Visiting Niagara Peninsula wineries from the USA side, you pass the fantastic Niagara Falls and on the Canadian side the not very pleasant tourist/honeymoon resorts of the type found at such great scenic pleasures around the world. Fortunately, the best show of the Falls is the illuminated one at night when you do not have to suffer the eyesore of tinsel-town. But don't let this one blink of visual pollution put you off visiting Ontario wineries; they are lovely people, the wines are good, and some of the Chardonnays excellent.

There is another interesting entry from the USA through the Detroit tunnel to Windsor, then proceed to Blenheim, a route that will embrace Ontario's south-western vineyards. This region contains more than fifty grape farms but less than a handful of wineries producing Chardonnay. Rieslings and the French hybrids are the dominant varieties. At this end of Ontario there is little sign of change.

Niagara Peninsula
The soils of this world-famous tourist area (which wine area in the world can rival the Niagara Falls?) are clay loams with little free lime problem. A rather unusual aspect is that most soils are tile-drained, Chardonnay being grown on the coarser soils with better natural drainage, but still tiled systematically at 8–10 metres with 10-centimetre tiles. I find this rather an exciting area, with enormous dedication to achieving world-class wines and a wonderful rapport between growers, makers and scientists. Notable producers are, in alphabetical order, Bright's, Château des Charmes and Inniskillan.

Nova Scotia

Agriculture Canada's research station, Kentville, on the peninsula province of Nova Scotia, has conducted grape trials continuously since 1913. But satisfactory wine grape types, mainly French hybrids, were not identified until the mid-1960s. With a renewed burst of enthusiasm in 1983, the station began a grape breeding programme with 2,000 seedlings under test. They realize that for a commercial winemaking future they must test more European winter-hardy varieties.

Chardonnay appears to have a bright future in Nova Scotia – a wine from Grand Pré Wines collected a Silver Medal in international competition in 1986. One swallow doesn't make a summer, but it certainly augurs well for the future. The only other farm winery at this time is the Jost Vineyard at Malagash.

The Chardonnay-lover with an interest in the unusual should keep an eye out for developments in Nova Scotia, as there are a number of large-scale plantings. Unfortunately, the 1986 vintage came after a season which had the lowest heat accumulation on record, but Nova Scotia can go forward with the knowledge of what can happen in a bad year – they do not have a lot to worry about.

AUSTRALASIA

By any measurable viticultural or oenological standards, the winemaker and wine consumer 'down-under' enjoy a very favoured status. This is brought about by almost ideal climatic conditions and a limited amount of political interference. This does not mean that there is not a variance between vintages or that yields are always ideal.

The grapegrower can grow exactly what and where he/she wants to grow. There is a winery at Alice Springs in the dry 'dead-heart' of Australia, while others are regularly covered with snow on the South Island of New Zealand. Nobody tells the individual how to prune, what the yield should be, or when the grapes can be picked. And, even more favourably than California which enjoys all of the above benefits, the 'down-under' producer can sell his wine to anyone, anywhere in the world straight from the vineyard.

Traditionally, the wineries of Australasia (and that includes New Zealand) have been 'fruit salad' producers – making every style of wine known to man: 'port', 'sherry', 'champagne', Riesling, 'claret', 'burgundy', 'Sauternes' and even Retsina. While this diversity of products and packages (the buyer has the choice of most products in regular bottles, flagons/2-litre jars or 4–5 litre 'casks' – the bag-in-the-box container affectionately known as 'Château Cardboard') is still maintained by the large national companies, the smaller and newer producers normally confine themselves to a couple of dry red and dry white varietals, and, maybe one speciality line such as a dessert or *méthode champenoise* wine.

Wine in Australia is grown in every state and under every conceivable climatic condition. The first grapes picked in the world during any vintage, and the longest growing season are both on the world's largest island and smallest continent. It is a fact that

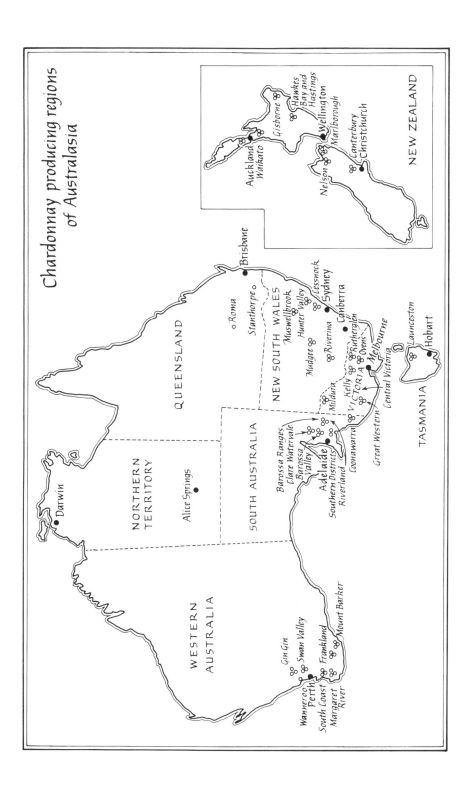

Chardonnay producing regions of Australasia

grapes for a particular vintage have been picked in the year before the vintage year even arrived! This came about by the early ripening in December of grapes normally harvested in January, yet in another state later maturing grapes were picked six months later.

It is about 3,000 kilometres from Brisbane to Adelaide, yet one does not have to travel any great distance – in a land of great distances – to go from one wine region to another. In many cases, not any further than in Europe. And Chardonnay is planted in each and every region, from the tropical high country of Queensland to the oft-frozen vineyards of Coonawarra. Such are the extremes.

The Great Dividing Range, while only 2,300 metres at its highest point, spears down the east coast of Australia from Cape York in northern Queensland to western Victoria, a distance of some 6,000 kilometres. A large percentage of Australia's premium vineyards are either on or within a coo-ee of this truly great range, whose existence plays a dominant part in the climatology of grape growing in eastern Australia.

As will be seen in the Heat Summation chapter (see page 138), the elevation of a vineyard contributes significantly to the mesa-climate. The 1,000 metre elevation of southeast Queensland's vineyards, like those of west Texas, make it possible to grow first-class grapes. Two oddities here, the first being that the Queensland vineyards border a tropical rain-forest, and a nearby town is named, would you believe, Texas!

Grapes have been cultivated in Australia, with wildly fluctuating fortunes, since day one of British settlement two centuries ago. As Australasia is the only continent without indigenous vines, everything had to be taken there from distant lands. The original vines came from both South Africa and South America as potted plants, although the important collections of vines were brought to New South Wales from European vineyards by James Busby and, to a lesser extent, James MacArthur, early in the nineteenth century. These collections included the varieties 'Chardonnet' and white Pinot. From these nurseries vines of all types went to all parts of Australia.

As in all other countries, Chardonnay went through the misnomer problem until the last decade when it became generally recognized as Chardonnay, although a couple of diehards hang on to the Pinot tag. Until that time, Chardonnay had been called mainly white Pinot and was never treated seriously.

As usual, there are claims and counter-claims as to where the variety re-emerged as the 'great white hope', as it is so often named, in a country where Riesling was the popular classic – and white Burgundy was the drink for plebs; Australian white 'Burgundy' that is, made with every grape under the sun, including the Rhône red variety Syrah, without one drop of Chardonnay. Even today, Houghton's white 'Burgundy', made variously using Chenin, Muscadelle and Verdelho, is still the nation's number one selling white wine. Little wonder; as it is an excellent product regardless.

The Chardonnay renaissance came like an express train in the late 1970s and has been going flat-out ever since. And if any Australian wine product has captured the imagination of the export market, particularly the UK and USA, it is Chardonnay from down-under.

However, all this has created one enormous shambles in the vineyards. Chardonnay cuttings arrived from anywhere and everywhere as it came under demand right across this vast continent. The state departments of agriculture, commencing with Western Australia back in 1957, brought in cuttings from California and Europe. This has led to a situation where most growers have little idea of the origin of their vines.

All the same, there is little doubt in my mind that the modern day Chardonnay phenomenon started in the small central western NSW region of Mudgee. The 'white Pinot' had been in the Kurtz vineyard there as long as people can remember, but it took a strange twist of fate to bring it out into the open.

French ampelographers (those wonderul people who study grape vines) often visit the vineyards of the world including Australia. During the early 1960s one Dr Denis Boubals noted with considerable interest this so-called white Pinot growing in the Kurtz Mudgee vineyard and put this information into his memory bank. His Australian tour was so strenuous that, by the time of arrival in Mildura, the provincial capital for the vast Sunraysia wine-producing region, Boubals was ordered to hospital. On learning of this situation, the renowned viticulturist Bob Hollick took the ailing Frenchman into his home and under the protective care of a loving family. On recovery, Boubals was so moved that he wanted to give the family a lasting present, and what better than a viticultural gem. He told Hollick of his discovery of the grape vine which produced the world's best white wines, and not only that – the vines were virus free and the best examples he had seen anywhere! But the most unbelievable aspect of this generosity was that the vines were from the pre-phylloxera era, one of the few such existing vineyards in the entire world.

Hollick broke all records getting to Mudgee and signing a three year agreement for the supply of cuttings from the quarter acre plot of Chardonnay. These originally went into the Mildara vineyards and subsequently into the Sunraysia commercial nurseries, some of the largest in Australia. It is impossible to keep these sorts of discoveries under wraps, so from here the Chardonnay went to all corners of the nation.

One obvious question is how did these vines get to the Kurtz vineyard. That in itself is another interesting story. It appears that they came from the long-defunct Penrith NSW area and the Kaluna vineyards of Colin Laraghy in the 1930s. Laraghy was purchasing grapes in Mudgee and took cuttings there to help improve the blend of the white wines. These were originally planted at the Craigmoor vineyard, then taken to Roth's, then subsequently to the Kurtz property. Where Laraghy got his original cuttings is a matter of considerable conjecture although Penrith is not far from the original MacArthur vineyards. Yet, another more likely source would be the Hunter Valley Distillery vineyards of Penfold's. *Sacré bleu*, Chardonnay going into a distillery!

Be that as it may, the Chardonnay rage started very quietly down-under, with a few offerings from Craigmoor of Mudgee and Tyrrell's of Pokolbin in the Hunter Valley. Tyrrell's have gone on to great things, their wine being recognized in all the major markets of the world. Craigmoor has kept a rather low profile, suffering nothing in quality; in fact the first wines of the early 1970s are still in splendid condition. Pieter van Gent, who made those first wines, recalls the period as being one when all and sundry were cautious and nervous about the great white hope. Little did we know what was ahead!

South Australia

More like New South Wales (NSW) with its limited number of clearly defined large wine areas, South Australia emerged as the nation's number one wine-producing state following the phylloxera devastation of most of the NSW and Victorian vineyards just prior to the end of last century.

Rightfully called 'The Wine (or Festival) State', South Australia is the driest state on earth's driest continent. It is something of a paradox that wine, coupled with tourism, is by far the State's biggest dollar earner. And coupled they are, for the wine areas are the principal tourist attractions.

Not only does South Australia have quantity (something like 62 per cent of the national production), but it has a depth of quality that stands alone. This is not to say that great wines are not made in other states – they are – but nowhere near the volume of South Australia. Also, South Australia has a wide range of climates and geography, plus winemaking skills in abundance, to provide every type of Chardonnay from the world's best to the cheapest non-wooded styles.

Barossa Valley

This area is host to such internationally known companies as Penfold's/Kaiser Stuhl, Orlando, Seppelt's, Yalumba (Hill Smith Estate), Saltram and Wolf Blass, all major participants in the Chardonnay stakes, most with several labels.

Barossa wineries process about three times the amount of fruit grown locally, drawing grapes from any number of regions around Australia. Fruit or juice is brought from such faraway places as Coonawarra, 400 kilometres to the southeast, and even the Hunter Valley in New South Wales, more than 1,000 kilometres distant. However, the largest volume of fruit comes from the adjoining bountiful Riverland region. Add to this the Valley's own geo-graphical complexities ranging from the warm Valley floor to the 500–600 metre East Barossa Ranges where snow often covers the vineyards. Within the Valley itself there is as much as five weeks' difference between the first and last picking of Chardonnay. Thus, it quickly becomes apparent that Barossa offers the winemaker a wide choice of fruit to work with.

Without question, the relatively low cost and abundance of this fruit places the Australian wine consumer, and the country's export customers, in the favoured position of being able to afford top-class Chardonnays from such notable makers as Orlando and Seppelt's, in particular. These wines are well known in both the UK and US markets as being exceptional value for money. Sadly, the UK consumer is saddled with unbelievably crippling taxes which almost doubles the US price for a similar commodity.

While growers in the NSW wine areas of Mudgee and Hunter generally have similar philosophies in making Chardonnay, the Barossa makers use methods which vary dramatically from one winery to the next. And this applies to the full spectrum of manipulative practices that can be used, from the choice of yeast to oak casks.

As the phylloxera louse never did visit the South Australian vineyards, an impenetrable barrier of controls was invoked on the importing of grape vines into the State until well into the 1970s. This left South Australia as a later starter in the Chardonnay handicap, but in traditional style they are running a great race and quickly making up lost ground.

This most important of Australian wine regions, Barossa, has a very interesting background, having been named after a Spanish region due to the alleged similarity of the country, and settled by Silesian Lutherans who were encouraged to settle by an Englishman. A number of today's wine companies are headed by descendants of those original Silesians, and the Lutheran church plays a dominant role in every little community. There is such a thing as 'Barossa Deutsch' and it is not hard to find such German delicacies in the bakers' shops as Hönigkuchen, Quarkkuchen or Streuselkuchen, while the butchers proudly display their home-made Mettwurst, Blutwurst and Leberwurst. German-born and trained winemakers have long been coming to the Valley and one, Wolfgang Blass, has transformed the face of winemaking in Australia. Yet, as a Chardonnay maker, his product is confined to cellar door sales and export. His nationally distributed wine of this style is a Semillon-Chardonnay blend, known as Classic Dry White.

One of the British exceptions to the German 'occupation' is the Yalumba/Hill Smith stronghold at Angaston. Established 140 years ago by a Dorset brewer with that awfully common name of Smith, Yalumba ('all the land around') is not only recognized as one of the nation's top wineries, but as a bastion of all things British – cricket, thoroughbred racing, art and even polo has slipped in with the current sixth generation. Tiger shooting was another family pastime during the third generation!

But it is the wine magic of the Barossa Valley that brings many thousands of people from all over the globe every odd numbered year to one of the world's most spectacular wine festivals – the Barossa Vintage Festival.

Playing a leading role in viticultural development in Australia is the Barossa Valley Research Station. Nearby is Roseworthy Agriculture College, the nation's oldest oenology and viticulture school and an important contributor to Australia's wine quality.

Leading Chardonnay producers, other than those mentioned

above are: Basedow's, Heggies, Krondorf, Mount Adam, Rose-worthy College and Leo Buring.

Riverland

Most of the giants of the Australian winemaking industry have large holdings in this rather arid area, where the annual rainfall is twelve inches. Little fruit is processed in the area other than by Consolidated Co-operatives, well known in both the UK and USA under their Renmano and Berri labels. Angoves is another local producer with national distribution and some exports. But the largest amount of fruit and juice is taken to processing facilities elsewhere, mainly the Barossa Valley. Rarely is this made into a regional wine, rather it is blended with fruit from other areas. This practice highlights the difference between the European appel-lation system and the freedom enjoyed by the New World pro-ducer. The New World winemaker is trying to make the best wine possible by blending regions rather than being tied to making the best wine possible from local fruit.

McLaren Vale

Almost in the outer suburbs of Adelaide, this classic red wine area now produces the epitome of what Chardonnay is all about. Just as with the red wines, the Chardonnays are mouth-filling with clearly defined flavours of melon, grapefruit and stone fruits. These wines are not 'whisperers', or even delicate; rather they have something to say which can be heard by even the very hard of hearing.

Unlike the Barossa, which does not have its own regional Chardonnay flavour due to its expansive geography, without introducing the imported fruit to further complicate its character, McLaren Vale uses mostly local fruit prepared by local growers.

Leaving aside the large Hardy organization, who anyhow bring most of their fruit from distant Padthaway, the region is made up of mainly small to medium sized producers who still market national-ly and internationally. However, Hardy's are an important part of the region, and, although the fruit is not local, the winemaking and finishing is 100 per cent so. The suburban nature of the Vale is such that it cannot cater for vineyards of the size needed by an organization like Hardy's. Still, in my opinion, the Hardy Collec-tion (Padthaway) Chardonnay is right in there with the Seppelt's and Orlando RF, representing, by any standards, superb value for

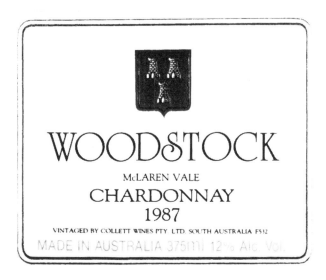

money wines. The 'Eileen Hardy' Chardonnay label is the top of the range product.

Other McLaren Vale labels which will bring joy to overseas and local consumers are: Chais Clarendon, Château Reynella, d'Arenberg, Middlebrook, Wirra Wirra and Woodstock.

A little to the south of McLaren Vale is the Currency Creek vineyard, another winery with an outstanding Chardonnay.

Coonawarra

Due to the excellence of its red wines, Coonawarra has long been known as the Bordeaux of Australia. In what is probably the world's lowest heat summation region (cooler than either Bordeaux or Burgundy) for growing commercial quantities of red wine, it is only reasonable to expect that the classic white varieties, Riesling and Chardonnay, would flourish. Yet white wine grapes have only been seriously cultivated for the last decade of their century-long existence. As it is in the Clare region, Riesling is the number one favourite in Coonawarra, regardless of its unpopularity in the market place. In recent years, Chardonnay has been reluctantly accepted, but not before many had tried their luck with Sauvignon (blanc), which was a bit of a flop.

Having accepted that the public wants Chardonnay, the region, lead by big-boys, Wynn's and Mildara, has responded strongly with some outstanding wines. Much of the juice and fermented wines is taken elsewhere for finishing, as none of the large companies who dominate the area have bottling or ageing facilities in Coonawarra.

Also, most large companies have extensive vineyard commitments in the Keppoch-Padthaway region some 80 kilometres to the north. Some of this fruit is brought to Coonawarra for initial processing, then forwarded to the Barossa Valley, McLaren Vale or even neighbouring Victoria for finishing. In many cases, the fruit itself is shipped hundreds of kilometres to the wineries. Large vineyard holdings exceeding 100 hectares each in the area are held by Seppelt's – the pioneers – Hardy's, Lindeman's/Leo Buring and Penfold's/Wynns.

Hardy's crush grapes and take the juice to Reynella, and the others have crushing and fermenting facilities in the Coonawarra. The other major player, Mildara, has its vineyards, fermenting and ageing facilities at Coonawarra, but the wine is taken to the company's north-west Victorian base, Merbein, for packaging.

As could be expected, the Chardonnays of Coonawarra show the typical citrus characters associated with cool growing regions, although the warmer Padthaway fruit introduces flavours such as melon, stone and tropical fruits.

While the big-boys make outstanding Chardonnays, a fact increasingly recognized around the world, the small family producers are no less capable. It is purely a matter of personal taste. The following are the names of some, all top quality: Bowen Estate, Brand's, Hollick's and Katnook.

Other South Australian Regions

While the Clare and Adelaide Hills regions have their own rightful place in the Australian wine industry, in terms of size, neither is a big Chardonnay producer. That in no way detracts from the quality of Chardonnay made there. As demonstrated in the Beaune and London tastings the Petaluma wine held its own with the best. The Petaluma winery is located at Piccadilly in the Adelaide Hills, and the fruit coming from other places, mainly Coonawarra.

The Clare region has long had a love affair with the Riesling grape and, as a general rule, has snubbed Chardonnay in favour of the German variety. This lack of local competitiveness is apparent from the styles of wines produced, although one hopes that better things are just around the corner. Wolf Blass and the century-old

Stanley Wine Co. (now Hardy-owned following the recent purchase from baked bean producer H. I. Heinz) are the main Chardonnay producers.

New South Wales

Hunter Valley

One could say that the Hunter Valley is the ultimate Chardonnay enigma. It is the hottest, and possibly the wettest, viticultural climate on earth, but produces world-class Chardonnays. Although there may be some doubt about the wet climate bit, their can be none about the wine quality. Again and again, the Tyrrell's and Rosemount Chardonnays (just to select two – there must be at least twenty other excellent producers) have proved their class in all types of judgings, by all sorts of people, right around the globe.

The Hunter Valley, along with much of the rest of Australia's east coast, is semi-tropical, and avocados, bananas and pineapples abound, though not in the grape-growing areas. The winters are relatively dry but in summer, monsoons deluge the vineyards, occasionally right at harvest time. This causes all sorts of viticultural problems, not the least being the necessity to spray more than usual against mildew and botrytis.

Despite this, in many ways the Hunter can claim to being the centre of Chardonnay production down-under. Certainly, as an

I 9 8 7
HUNTER VALLEY
CHARDONNAY

PRODUCT OF AUSTRALIA
750 ML 12.0% ALC/VOL

area, it combines the largest planting of the variety, and was probably the first area to commercialize Chardonnay upon its emergence as a varietal wine.

Maybe these oddities of climate, and Chardonnay's good behaviour in such a place, give some credence to the proposition that the variety is from a warm-hot birthplace rather than a cold climate such as Burgundy's?

In what is known locally as the 'upper' Hunter, Rosemount Estates orchestrates three very successful Chardonnay labels: the top-of-the-line Roxburgh, named after its vineyard of origin, the international favourite Show Chardonnay and the regular release Yellow Label. These typify the extremes of winemaking styles, the first two being barrel-fermented and the latter made in stainless steel and finished in oak. These treatments are reflected in the respective retail prices of the wines.

Much the same applies at Tyrrell's and at Wyndham Estate with their different labels, although Tyrrell's has the biggest proportion of barrel-fermented wines. Tyrrell's is also one of the few Australian producers which has a preference for wild vineyard yeasts rather than bought-in cultures or other yeast forms.

A very interesting Hunter innovation is the blend of Semillon and Chardonnay. As yet it is not taken seriously, but with the shortage and cost of straight Chardonnay, I hope consumers worldwide will take a serious look at this marvellous accommodation of two splendid varieties. I have no reservations about the two parts making a better wine than either of the individual components, albeit with a couple of years neccessary before the wines' marriage is consummated.

In a region where Chardonnay is widespread and produced with almost equal excellence, it is extremely difficult to recommend just a few names. But the following labels, other than those named above, are more likely to be known in international markets: Hungerford Hill, McWilliam's, Robson, Rothbury Estate, Lindeman's, Saxonvale and Tulloch's. No less excellent, but more likely to be found in the Australian market are Allandale, Allanmere, Arrowfield, Darson, Fraser, Lake's, Little's, Mount View, Peterson's, Sutherland and Terrace Vale.

Mudgee

Mainly through the efforts of the region's largest producer, Montrose Wines, the 'nest in the hills', as Mudgee translates from the native tongue, is becoming a hot item on the international Chardonnay market. Lead by Montrose, which sells under the 130-year-old Craigmoor label and the more youthful Amberton label, a number of other superb Chardonnay makers are reinforcing the international standing of the Mudgee region.

Although on the central western slopes of the Great Dividing Range, Mudgee is still influenced in some years by summer monsoons, but is far more likely to enjoy winter rains than the Hunter region. This sets the regions apart climatically, yet many of the same winemaking philosophies are employed bringing the Chardonnay styles of the two neighbouring regions closer together. Mudgee fruit is keenly sought by Hunter producers.

Craigmoor, under a different owner and winemaker, Pieter van Gent, probably made Australia's first commercial Chardonnay back in the early 1970s. Craigmoor, now with a relatively low profile, continues to make a wonderful drop or three of its traditional Chardonnay in a leaner style than its big brother, Montrose. Former Craingoor winemaker/consultant Barry Platt has acquired fruit from a neighbouring vineyard, Seldom Seen, and is now producing a Chardonnay under that label along with his own at his winery in the quaint mining town of Gulgong (the town featured on the Australian ten-dollar bill). Having also acquired the Hill of Gold winery and vineyards, Barry Platt and

Château de Fuissé – a jewel in southern Burgundy. Supreme quality at half the price of top Côte d'Or Chardonnay equivalents (*Mick Rock/Cephas*)

Relatives Christian de Billy (President) and Christian Pol Roger (Director-General) of Champagne Pol Roger evaluate their outstanding Blanc de Blancs

Cramant – one of the 'Grand Cru' Chardonnay villages along the Côte des Blancs, home of Champagne's best Chardonnay (*Claude Huyghens and Françoise Danrigal*)

The source of much conjecture in Burgundy – and still to be proven – high trellising at Nantoux, Hautes Côtes de Beaune (*Mike Rock/Cephas*)

Wines from Corton-Charlemagne, Batard-Montrachet, Chassagne-Montrachet mature quietly in Moillard's cellars, Nuits-St-Georges (*Mick Rock/Cephas*)

A commitment to ancient viticultural traditions and modern winemaking techniques are the aims of Villa Banfi here in Tuscany, Italy (*Mick Rock/Cephas*)

Italy's Alto Adige region is spearheading that country's Chardonnay drive. Christof (*left*) and Herbert Tiefenbrunner are in the vanguard (*Mick Rock/Cephas*)

No more old wooden casks
to hold back Spanish white
wine endeavours; a sample
is drawn from a stainless
steel tank (*Mick Rock/Cephas*)

Pupitres loaded with Cava
Chardonnay await riddling
at Codorníu, the world's
largest maker of sparkling
wine, just north of
Barcelona
(*Mick Rock/Cephas*)

Modern as tomorrow: uniquely designed, Rosemount winery set in the Australian bushland. Technology and excellence go hand in hand

Paniers à vendages – traditional Burgundy. On the Hautes Côtes and the Côtes d'Or grapes are picked and transported in these baskets
(*Mick Rock/Cephas*)

Designed to perpetuate the Spanish heritage of California wine, the Robert
Mondavi winery, Oakville, is a major tourist attraction

World beaters! George Fistonich and Kym Milne (winemaker), Villa Maria,
New Zealand, celebrate best Chardonnay, International Wine competition,
Bristol 1987

Chardonnay: queen of white grape varieties (*Mick Rock/Cephas*)

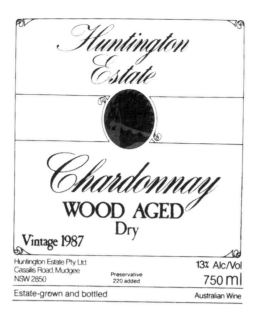

company are destined to play an important part in the future welfare of Mudgee wine.

Huntington Estates and owner Bob Roberts have been marketing their blockbuster reds and Chardonnay in the international market place for a decade or more. I must admit to a sneaking passion for these incredible products.

One of the features of winemaking in New South Wales over the past decade has been the overall improvement in the general standard. Gone are the 'seat-of-the-pants' old brigade of family winemakers to be replaced by young professionally trained and, in many cases, internationally experienced winemakers. Foremost among these is Ian McRae at the Miramar winery – despite its name it is about 200 kilometres from any ocean. With strong skills right across the winemaking (and do-it-yourself) board, McRae was a pioneer among the Semillon-Chardonnay producers and still has a number of back vintages of excellent Chardonnays and blends. Certainly a name to be filed away by the Chardonnay aficionado.

Of considerable interest to the health conscious is the Botobolar winery, which is organically farmed by the Wahlquist family. It is a worthwhile exercise to compare the Botobolar Chardonnay with those developed using the various sprays employed for weed, insect and fungicide control.

In all, Mudgee is a different wine town with a strong agricultural base. It is friendly, homely and a wonderful place to visit.

Murrumbidgee Irrigation Area

Unlike the highly productive central California wine regions, where Chardonnay production is relatively small, the vast inland wine areas of Australia – the Murrumbidgee irrigation area (MIA), Sunraysia on the New South Wales/Victorian border and the Riverland area of South Australia – are truly important areas for Chardonnay production. Not only is wine made and bottled under local labels in these three areas, but huge quantities of fruit, juice and wine are taken to many other regions, ranging from the Hunter Valley in New South Wales to the Barossa Valley in South Australia.

A unique feature of these areas is the absolute division between grapegrowing and winemaking. As a general rule, the grower produces the fruit and the makers do not get involved in the vineyard – a situation unlike most other regions. The importance of these three regions can be gauged by the massive contribution to the State's total grape yields, the MIA producing about 80 per cent of the New South Wales total, the Riverland about 70 per cent of the South Australia total, and Sunraysia a figure thereabout for Victoria.

The two major local MIA producers are McWilliam's of Hunter fame and San Bernadino. While both have national distribution in Australia and wide exports throughout the Pacific region, McWilliam's tends to stick with the UK market and San Bernadino is strongly entrenched in North America. Both makers tend to rely on almost unwooded fruit flavours and are aimed at the low-middle priced market, the exceptions in the Chardonnay field as almost all Australian wines have some oak cask treatment.

Victoria

More than a century ago the colony of Victoria was known in wine circles as John Bull's vineyard. Today the State calls itself 'The Garden State' for no obvious reason. At last count there was something approaching 100 wineries, scattered almost the entire length and breadth of the nation's smallest mainland state, but 90 per cent of all the wine comes from only five major producers. This centralization of power means that the other ninety-five or so wineries are 'penny packets', unable to be categorized into any substantial regions despite many efforts. However, these small producers pack a hefty wallop when it comes to wine quality.

By far the largest volume (over 80 per cent) of fruit comes from the Sunraysia district centred on the attractive Murray River provincial city of Mildura. Major players in the Chardonnay game here are Mildara and Lindeman's, who both service international markets, with Fitzpatrick Estate being a high volume producer for other labels, and to a much lesser extent, their own label. Further up the River towards the Australian Alps can be found the Tisdall Winery at Echuca, Seppelt's Barooga vineyard and the Morris winery at Rutherglen, all distinguished names and products. Not far from Rutherglen is the Brown family operation at Milawa, a name well known in international markets. On the road to Melbourne are the Goulburn Valley/central Victoria regions where one will find such notable Chardonnay producers as Château Tahbilk and Mitchelton, near the small town of Nagambie. A little further to the west and on top of the Range is Knight's Granite Hills, a family quickly enhancing their red wine fame with some outstanding Chardonnays. Not far from Melbourne airport, at the century-old Craiglee vineyard, Pat Carmody is reviving the splendour of this famous vineyard with a top Chardonnay.

Only about forty-five minutes east of Melbourne is the much-publicized Yarra Valley where Moët & Chandon are establishing the Australian counterpart to their outstanding Napa Valley property, Domaine Chandon. In the hills around this former dairy and vineyard region can be found several fine examples of the Chardonnay craft – but don't look for bargains! Well, maybe they are bargains, but not at the low-medium price range. Coldstream Hills, Yarra Burn, Lillydale and St Hubert's are spectacular wines for lovers of the essentially 'sur-lies' style.

On the way to Adelaide along the number 8 Duke highway, one will come to the one-blink town of Great Western (one blink and you've missed it!). But whatever you do, do not miss Great Western. Here you will find Best's, which caused much comment in the international Chardonnay judgings in London and Beaune. Also based here is the giant Seppelt's winemaking operation and 'champagne' cellars with two kilometres of underground caves, or 'drives' as they were called by the ex-goldminers who dug these underground cellars.

Seppelt's is a major flag carrier for Australian wines in the global scene and represents the best value of all Chardonnays overseas. Whereas Best's have but one label (of absolute top quality), Seppelt's at any one time seem to have at least three Chardonnays and fourteen bubbly labels including a blanc de blancs. Large volumes of fruit comes to this Seppelt's winery (they have two others in the Barossa Valley) from outstanding vineyards at Drumborg (about 400 tonnes) Victoria and Padthaway (about 2,000 tonnes) in South Australia.

Western Australia

Although there is not a large amount of Chardonnay planted in the 'State of Excitement', it is home to several leading international producers and an interesting source of information about the variety in Australia during recent times. Like South Australia, phylloxera did not visit the vineyards of the west, and this allows vinegrowers to plant cuttings without rootstocks. Despite all sorts of experiments, there is no evidence to suggest that Chardonnay benefits from growing on other than its own roots in Western Australia.

Immediately following the 1955 visit of Dr Harold Olmo from UC Davis, Chardonnay cuttings arrived in the west from California. While the Swan research station has a selection of cuttings, it appears as though most Chardonnay vines in the State came from the Houghton vineyards at Middle Swan, the source of almost all other varieties as well. Only twenty-five kilometres from downtown Perth, the Houghton vineyards and winery are 130 years old and embody the 'spirit of winemaking in the west'. The company has a large vineyard planting some fifty kilometres north at Gin Gin and operates another large spread nearly 300 kilometres away to the south at Frankland, giving it enormous fruit variety when coupled with their Swan Valley holdings. The resultant wines can only be described as superb. The only other Chardonnay producer of note in the valley is Westfield, and although small in size the Westfield Chardonnay is a giant in stature.

Down near the harbourside provincial capital of Albany is what is known locally as the Great Southern region. Here another outstanding West Australian Chardonnay is produced. Forest Hills is a truly stunning wine, but sadly produced in such limited quantities that it is devoured mainly by its own large following around Australia.

Along the sandy west coast is the vineyard/winery that gives the lie to any claims about the contribution of soils to wine quality. Will Nairn's Peel Estate vineyard is nothing but bottomless, golden beach sands with a dash of limestone. From this frivolous piece of soil/sand (call it what you like) comes some of the nation's best Cabernet Sauvignon, Rhône-style Syrah and a very well-made Chardonnay. Anyone with at least an ounce of belief in the contribution of soil to wine quality – as opposed to wine structure – should bring their bucket and spade to this site and build a few sand-castles while enjoying some of the world's truly great wines. Another eighty kilometres south at Capel Vale, art-loving radiologist Peter Pratten is doing similar things with Chardonnay in an old riverbed.

By international standards, the real strength of West Australian Chardonnay is a further seventy kilometres to the southwest, centred on the town of Margaret River.

Margaret River

It was not until the 1960s that vines were planted in this area, with Chardonnay not making an appearance until the mid-1970s. As such, Margaret River could be classified as a 'new' area, but its achievements in only twenty-five years have been monumental. I think that these achievements signal a number of very strong messages to the rest of the winemaking world: that tradition has a very small role to play in wine quality, and that community spirit and the desire to succeed, coupled with an amenable climate, can overcome almost every obstacle. The iron stone gravelly sands surely make folly of any argument about soils and their contribution to quality.

It is anything but plain sailing in this windy part of the world. Yields are low, brought about by the equinoxtial gales at flowering and fruit set time. Also the strong sea breeze known in days past as the 'trade winds', coming in from the Indian Ocean, carries a lot of damaging salt with it. Then there are the birds, the flying type who just wait until the vinegrower's annual work is almost complete before they swoop in and take the lot; or, at least, a good portion.

While one can take nothing away from the present practitioners for their skills and dedication, once again that man Robert Mondavi appears centre stage. In the early days of Margaret River, Mondavi was involved as a consultant to a group of Americans who had a portion of the action at Leeuwin Estate before the Horgan family purchased all the shares. Mondavi influenced the purchase of equipment and the winemaking philosophy at a time when few people in Australia had ever heard of Chardonnay. In addition, there was substantial input from the Robert Mondavi Winery in

Oakville, California; Bob himself was right there feeding grapes into the crusher at the furthest point on earth from his home! Leeuwin Estate, and other Margaret River Chardonnays, have gone on to become if not the world's best, certainly in the front rank.

To the eternal credit of Leeuwin Estate they denied nothing, least of all pouring money into a bottomless pit, in the search for excellence. It is the highest priced Australian white wine and was the second highest priced wine in my international judgings. Leeuwin Estate unashamedly say that they are trying to make French-style wines. My impression is that they have succeeded in making a rich, complex international-style wine with classic Australian overtones rather than a French look-alike. Much the same can be said for the majority of producers in the region lead by Diana Cullen, 1987 Australasian Winemaker of the Year, who have adopted the 'sur-lies' style with a number of individual variations.

Both Cullens and Leeuwin Estate wines can be found in the major markets of the world, in London, New York and even Hong Kong – a long way from this remote corner of the globe where to the south the nearest land mass is the Antarctic and to the west, South Africa.

Tasmania and Queensland

Despite being well over 2,000 kilometres apart the vineyards of Launceston Piper's Brook in northern Tasmania and Stanthorpe in south-east Queensland share a number of similarities. Both areas are isolated, small and good.

The future of Chardonnay in Tasmania was given the golden seal of approval when the famous Reims Champagne house, Roederer, entered a joint venture with local producer Heemskerk. Obviously this gave the region a terrific shot-in-the-arm and also raised a few eyebrows. The straight Heemskerk Chardonnay, away from the bubbly material, is a fine wine, as is nearby neighbour Piper's Brook.

On a spectacular site above the Derwent River north of Launceston can be found Marion's Vineyard with a Chardonnay equal to the scenery. And that is it for Tasmania.

Nestling right up on top of the Great Dividing Range, almost on the New South Wales – Queensland border, the Chardonnay lover with tons of grit and determination can find some really remote wines. The Robinson Family wine is tried and true, and in recent years has been followed (between frosts) by Bungawarra, Rumbalara and Sundown Valley.

Chardonnay in Australia has come a long way. Its adaptability in near desert country, snow-covered vineyards and mountain heights proves it worth to the grower and consumer. To master these vagaries of geography and climate, there is a long way to go yet. Hopefully, there are even better things to come . . .

New Zealand

When the Villa Maria Estate's New Zealand Chardonnay won the double Gold Medal at the 1987 International Wine and Spirits competition in the UK against all-comers, the happening signalled to the world at large that 'down-under' was, in fact 'on top'. Plus a few other important messages. It was not so much a matter of whether an Australasian wine would win, but, rather, which one?

While Chardonnay is a late arrival on the 'shakey islands', along with Sauvignon (blanc), it has found a natural home. These two varieties have performed outstandingly in all major viticultural areas. McWilliam's, then an off-shoot of the famous Australian company, brought the first vines into the country early in the 1970s, but by 1975 the Viticultural Research Unit did not have a single vine. But, despite the late start, it was only a decade before New Zealand was right there with the world's best, if one is looking for real Chardonnay flavour.

The country's biggest producer, Montana, well known in international markets, set the ball rolling with a stunning 1976 Gisborne wine which was my introduction to a continuing line of fine wines, in most cases unwooded. Nearly all the early Kiwi wines were unwooded, or contained just a gentle kiss of oak. The Montana, and also McWilliam's wines, developed well over six to seven years, building palate weight, fattening out, picking up colour, but remaining firm with (and because of) good acidity. New oak treatment became a part of the Montana wine only in later vintages, such as 1986 and 1987.

The Gisborne region on the North Island's east coast, which was devastated by floods just prior to the 1988 vintage, is the largest Chardonnay producing region and the source of fruit for well-known companies such as Cook's, who featured in the London and Beaune tastings, and the aforementioned Villa Maria.

Further down the coast is Hawkes Bay, a name to be carefully filed away by wine lovers the world over. To me anyhow this is the artistic heart of New Zealand winemaking, and its 'Mediterranean' maritime climate produces magnificent fruit year in, year out. The Villa Maria associate company, Vidals, is located here and makes a range of Chardonnays from local fruit. Both companies have 'Reserve' and lower ranked 'Private Bin' Chardonnays of note. The Reserve usually denotes a totally barrel-fermented and matured wine while the Private Bin range is a blend of stainless steel and oak fermented material. Many of the excellent 85s and 86s have been consumed as young wines, rather a pity as they have shown great complexity after a couple of years' bottle-age. Succeeding vintages have gone from strength to strength as the company's philosophy has been finalized and the winemaking team have become happy and confident with their work.

It was an ex-patriate Australian, John Hancock, now at Morton Estate, who led the way with barrel fermentation back in 1982. Using fruit from Hawkes Bay, Hancock has brought the Morton Estate Black Label to the forefront, in a country where the overall standard is excellent.

A lot of fruit from both Hawkes Bay and Gisborne is taken to wineries in and around West Auckland. Notable among these are the fine producers, Matua Valley and Collard Bros.

At the north end of the South Island is the spectacularly beautiful Marlborough region. Several of the big names in New Zealand winemaking can be found here, Montana and Corbans being to the fore, although most companies seem to receive some Marlborough fruit. Once again, much of this is taken to Auckland for processing, although Montana have a large commitment to the area in the way of processing facilities.

However, one local company, Hunter's, do everything for their estate-bottled wine right there. This outstanding wine, along with its Fumé Blanc and Sauvignon relatives, has a devoted band of followers in the UK and New York.

New Zealand winemaking is not confined to these major regions. The very joy for the wine tourist in 'instant Europe' is that wineries can be found almost everywhere, even on an island in Auckland Harbour! Many fine Chardonnays can be found in the West Auckland-Kumeu area, less than an hour's drive from the country's largest city. An hour driving south will bring the visitor to one of the world's finest hotel resorts, Hotel Du Vin, providing luxury in the middle of a vineyard and award-winning winery, De Redcliffe's Estate. Just north of the capital, Wellington, is the small but fast-moving Martinborough region, while close to the southern city of Christchurch can be found the Canterbury vineyards and Rugby grounds.

New Zealand may be isolated – it is a long way from Europe and north America – but I can assure the visitor that the wines will make the trip worthwhile. Why not start with a visit to your local wine shop?

ITALY

Trying to write an international book of this nature requires tons of input and co-operation from many people and organizations to compile and complete the many charts, diagrams and statistics that have not previously been gathered in one publication. There are two very positive statements, by Italians, about Italy generally: firstly, it is *not* possible!; secondly, it is *impossible*!

It is often very hard to work out which of these two standard answers is more acceptable. During one Italian visit, nothing was possible in my search for information, but on the positive side, everything was impossible! (Pierro Antinori excepted.)

Winemaking, in what could be considered as the 'home' of wine (seeing that they took the vine and its culture to France and Germany from where it spread to the rest of the world) to say the very least, is often highly traditional; on the other side of the coin, some of the world's best wine and winemaking equipment comes out of Italy.

All of the above is an enormous generalization as for twenty years or more I have been a lover of good Italian red wines. With the introduction of some French grape varieties – to blend with the local grapes – several Italian winemakers are crafting spectacular reds that are equal to the very best from any other country; simply outstanding. This has only come about by some visionary winemakers breaking away from the many traditional beliefs and philosophies that are so much a part of Italian winemaking – and, in some cases, even breaking the EEC/DOC laws. It is an interesting aside that those who have done it with reds are much the same people who are making the breakthrough with Chardonnay.

In both cases, the progressive development is not limited to any one area. It is almost nationwide, taking in the northeast and northwest and down through the centre of the country.

You will possibly note that mention has been made of the plethora and diversity of Burgundy appellations and labelling. This is kindergarten stuff by comparison with what the Italians have done with DOCs and labels.

In addition to the conventional, and not so conventional, still wines made from Chardonnay, a good portion of Chardonnay fruit is going into sparkling *méthode champenoise* wines. At this early stage of the Italian varietal white wine revolution, neither still nor sparkling wines are easy to obtain anywhere which may or may not be fortunate. In my opinion, there is certainly more consistency among the bubblies than the still wines. I would say that there is really not that much you can do to vary traditional *méthode* bubblies to any great extent: you either make it the traditional way or you don't. The bubbles themselves are the artistic expression. People do not seem to take the same liberties making sparklers as they are willing to do with the straight table wines. As pointed out elsewhere in this book, there is much one can do to vary the quality and flavour of table wines. It could be easily argued in an esoteric way that these variables are also there for sparklers, but most makers seem to stick with the straight and narrow path. I think this is a wonderful salute to Champagne.

The delightful wine journalist Jancis Robinson has described Italy as 'a hotbed of Chardonnay innovation' which is, indeed, generous. Maybe they are going through the learning curve of establishing Italian – north, central and elsewhere – styles. There appears to be a number of styles, even within regions, appearing all over the country which can be listed as:

1. The legal and illegal blends with Pinot Bianco (some DOC regulations do not allow such a blend).
2. The 'drink-now' styles which have found an enormous market in the USA, and other foreign markets at the lower end of the price range.
3. Attempts at a classical, non-wooded style expressing the full flavour of Chardonnay fruit alone.
4. A truly artistic style with previously unheard of barrel fermentation.

Travelling around the world a couple of times each year my central philosophy is to drink local wines wherever I may be, Missouri or Mâcon. It could be said that I am not a 'label-drinker' and this has opened up many wonderful experiences, often when least expected. Possibly this is the pleasure of discovery.

Admittedly, I buy at the lower end of the price range as, normally, I wish to have a bottle of *vino* with my food, not a memorable wine sensation every meal time. In this regard I have been disappointed with the Italian styles listed as 1. and 2. above. They are well-made wines, but I keep asking, 'Where's the flavour?' Even with California jug wines one can find some vinous flavours.

While the more artistic efforts are still in their early days and the makers still learning to match the fruit and oak, there are many encouraging signs coming from the north and centre of Italy.

Notable among producers in the Alto Adige and South Tyrol, facing the superb Dolomites, are Alois Lageder and Herbert Tiefenbrunner, both of whom have excellent track records with the local variety, Pinot Bianco.

On the northern side of the Apennines, just south of Bologna, is the Emilia-Romagna region, well known for its Sauvignon (blanc), Pinot Bianco and Riesling Italico. The Ministry of Agriculture does not even list Chardonnay as a variety, but despite the Ministry and EEC rules, Chardonnay will not be denied, albeit under a generic label.

A little to the southwest, Frescobaldi is determined to become a leader. While their products enjoyed some success with the Beaune panel in the international evaluations, the UK panel did not rate it very highly. (Nor did this writer.)

About 130 kilometres north of Rome is the province of Umbria where there are two major Chardonnay producers – the 600-year-old family company, Antinori, and Lungarotti. Although there are only small plantings (about 115 hectares at the time of writing) all

the natural assets are in place for a rosy future. In view of Antinori's quantum leap forward in red wines since they blended Cabernet Sauvignon with local varieties, it would be fair to anticipate something equally spectacular with Chardonnay once they have had more experience with the variety.

Other producers to look out for in the central and southern regions of Italy are Capezzana and the enormous Villa Banfi.

In the northwest, not far from Turin in the heart of Piedmont country, the renowned Angelo Gaja is weaving a similar type of magic into Chardonnay that has previously made him one of the most sought-after red winemakers in Europe. But Gaja is not the only one to make inroads into the new field of Chardonnay in Piedmont; an equally famous neighbour, Pio Cesare, has also made the switch with a degree of success.

The producers of Italy are being ably supported in their endeavours by several research stations around the country. The Istituto Sperimentale per la Viticoltura at Conegliano are producing a handbook on five grapes, which includes Chardonnay, and the station is also well into rootstock trials. All in all, the Italian scene is exciting, and Chardonnay-lovers should keep a watchful eye on happenings there. It is a sad fact of life that the value of the Italian lira nowadays lifts their wine prices out of the 'cheap' category. They are going to have a big fight on their hands to stay in the value-for-money category when compared to the offerings from the New World. However, the wine lover can decide this for him/herself after completing my suggested Chardonnay tasting on page 15.

SPAIN

Very much like Italy, Spanish winemaking has traditionally depended on local varieties rather than the universal favourites such as Cabernet Sauvignon, Chardonnay and Riesling. In recent years there has been a re-think of this philosophy by the more progressive producers in both countries and it is of considerable interest to note that Cabernet and Chardonnay have been used to bolster local varieties in new blends. Several of these wines, more particularly the Cabernet blends of Torres in Spain and Antinori in Italy, have produced wines of unbelievable beauty. The same cannot be said of the Chardonnay blends which have produced only slightly above average wines, by my standards. Surely, the Torres Gran Viña Sol White Label blend of Parellada and Chardonnay are very pleasant wines with a large following around the world, but not destined to achieve the greatness of a straight, classical Chardonnay.

Unfortunately, Spanish producers have not, as yet, been seduced by this great white variety. In fact, it took former Catalan, but now Beverley Hills restaurateur Jean Leon, to buy some land and make the first international-style Spanish Chardonnay, albeit in the California rather than Burgundy mould. The Jean Leon wines have been variously called 'whoppers', 'fat', 'buttery' and all those other epithets associated with the California Chardonnays of old.

But these are early days yet and the future promises many good things, with the central stage being in the Penedés area, not far from the pulsating city of Barcelona. Here the geography allows for maritime and mountain climates and, with well-drained soils, the future is limitless.

In the adjoining province of Lerida, gigantic things are happening. The Raventos family who own the massive Codorníu cava,

have undertaken one of the most amazing vineyard developments the world has seen this century at their Raimat estate. A channel nearly 200 kilometres long has been built to carry water from the Pyrenees to this desert-like arid country where 300 hectares of Chardonnay is grown along with another 500 hectares of noble varieties and a healthy smattering of local vines. This vast amount of carefully irrigated vineyard provides bountiful quantities of fruit for both still and sparkling Chardonnays.

The still wine appears under the Raimat label; some sparkling Raimat is made in nearby Penedés but the bulk goes to Codorníu for the famous Champenois – Codorníu Chardonnay – a real challenge to the French-Champenois. Until 1992 the wine also carries a *Méthode Traditionelle Champenoise* tag. French may be the name, but the massive vineyard and winery operations are straight California hi-tech. In the vineyards mechanical harvesting is the fast and efficient way to harvest, and frost protection comes from spray systems that automatically start work when the temperature drops below freezing. Similar systems are used in Australia.

This is all a bit up-market for the average Spanish grower who provides the bodega with more than 80 per cent of its grape needs. Slowly, the growers, bodega, climatologists and other interested parties are starting to talk between themselves, and the future for this part of Spain and Chardonnay looks very bright.

PART THREE

Chardonnay in the Vineyard

Soils

Although the chemistry used today may seem complex, the wine-making process is absurdly simple. Fill a bucket with grapes and the weight will break the skin of the berries at the bottom, liberating their juice. Wild yeasts which occur in the grapes' waxy skin will soon begin the fermentation process which transforms juice into wine. It is a completely natural process and even with the complex systems used in modern wineries, the essence of the operation is as it was thousands of years ago. Yet when it comes to winemaking many myths abound.

One winemaking myth is that the 'famous' soils of Burgundy, Barossa, Champagne, or Sonoma contribute a great deal to wine quality. 'These unique soils exist only in X, Y and Z and make our wines so much better, and impossible to copy,' we are assured. Perhaps the most classic lines on this subject come from the book *The Soul of Wine* by Constantin-Weyer: 'A secret alchemy works upon even the least of the soil's riches to produce an elixir beyond compare.'

Of all the fallacies and romantic distortions disseminated about wine, the soil/quality relationship is by far the most misleading and heavily promoted. It is for this reason that I now include a chapter on soil – dealing with its make-up, variations, strengths and faults – in the hope that the reader will be able to make some worthwhile conclusions about such extravagant claims.

Chardonnay grapes grown on the gravelly, sandy soils of south-western Australia will make a different, but equally as good wine as the best from Burgundy's Kimmeridgian limestone or marlstone soils, or the rich clay loams of Napa. What will be different is the viticultural contribution to the structure of the wine. During the processing of the grape juice and must (unfinished wine), the winemaker has a number of manipulative tools (discussed in Part Four of this book) to alter this structure – and the perceived quality of the finished wine.

Certainly, soil is one of the primal needs for growing first-class grapes – the principal requirement for making first-class wine; grapevines also need air, light and water. But regardless of what any old wives' tales or national folklore would have us believe, no one single climate or soil is the most suitable of all. There are, instead, a wide range of both suitable soils and climates. The grapevine is a most adaptable plant, thriving from Bulgaria to Brazil – and no variety is more adaptable than Chardonnay, the ultimate gadabout. As Anthony Hanson says in his superb book, *Burgundy*, 'No one factor accounts for quality, variety or character, for there are as many factors as there are cards in a pack. Each vineyard is dealt a different hand, and every year the cards are shuffled. Nor have we discussed the Joker in the deck, man. The part he plays will make or mar the game.'

Terroir

During the mid-1980s, a battle, fuelled by a very articulate California winemaker, raged back and forth across the Atlantic about the merits of Bordeaux soil and its contribution to wine quality. The point at issue was the Bordelais' long-held belief that the soil itself provided unique flavours and superior quality in a wine. Some of this hoo-ha can be attributed to a problem of translation: the word 'terroir' which we would translate as 'soil', has a far wider meaning in French.

Terroir is a combination of climate, soil and landscape which includes slope, drainage and texture, temperature by night and day, the number of hours the vines are exposed to sunlight, rainfall distribution, and a host of other factors. These are *combined* factors that affect the composition of the fruit, and ultimate wine quality – until such time as Anthony Hanson's Joker appears on the scene.

Like all plants, the vine grows best when its demands for air, light, water and nutrients are fully met. Today, a great deal is known about vine nutrition and the fertilizer industry has made it relatively simple to improve the supply of nutrients in deficient soils. In addition to supplying the fifteen mineral nutrients known to be necessary for healthy plant growth (nitrogen, phosphorus, potassium, sulphur, iron, calcium, magnesium, boron, manganese, copper, zinc, molybdenun, sodium, chlorine and cobalt) the soil also provides water and air, containing the much needed

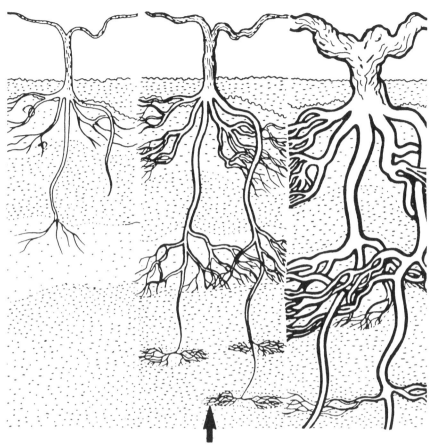

Fig. 6. A mature vine, about 15 years old. Its extensive root system penetrates deep into the soil to recover minerals and trace elements which will give its wine a characteristic flavour.

elements of hydrogen, oxygen and carbon (from carbon dioxide in the air).

The provision of these three elements depends largely on the physical condition of the soil. Grapevines, regardless of where they are grown, prefer soils that can supply moisture over the longest possible period, with the proviso that the soil should remain sufficiently well drained to avoid periodic oxygen deficiency arising from waterlogging of the roots. Even when waterlogging is minimal, root growth may be cut to half that of better aerated soils.

Such favourable conditions are not easy to find in Australian soils, owing to their age – some dating back 50 million years compared with the youthful 30,000-year-old soils of North America.

Root Systems

Grapevines respond to good physical soil conditions by developing vigorous roots that permeate the soil evenly and deeply, often to six metres or more. There is a strong body of evidence to suggest that deeply rooted vines will provide better quality fruit during times of abnormal weather (e.g. too much or too little rain). It is universally agreed that good soil structure is preferred to high soil fertility. Good structure allows for extensive root development and under these conditions fruit ripens earlier. It is also believed that the ripening period is longer and slower, producing fruit with more balanced chemical composition and flavour. Less suitable conditions may restrict root growth to two metres or less; in Champagne, not more than 0.5 metre.

The majority of fine feeding roots are found in the top 0.7 metres of soil, but the total depth of rooting seems to indicate relative root vigour. Nothing, however, alters the fact that the physical properties of soil either cannot be easily changed, or else are costly to change. Therefore, when new sites for vineyards are being considered, the soil's physical properties should be given prime consideration.

Soils are composed of five main components:

- mineral particles – the inorganic fraction, derived mainly from rocks by weathering but including animal skeletons and opal phytoliths from plants.
- organic materials – dead and decaying plants, animals and animal products.
- water – the 'soil solution' in which nutrient elements for plants are dissolved.
- air – which fills the voids between soil particles not filled by soil solution.
- living organisms – ranging in size from small animals to viruses.

Soils are different from one another because they have different proportions of these components. In addition, the components are arranged in different ways and, because the particles in their inorganic fractions have been affected to different degrees, have different size ranges and are made up of different minerals.

Most soils have a well-defined uppermost layer or top soil which merges sharply or gradually into other layers (horizons). The surface, subsoil and decomposing parent material horizons are designated the A, B and C horizons respectively. The various horizons may be differently coloured or have different textures, structures and other properties. This can be observed in road and rail cuttings or excavations.

Soils have been formed from rocks and sediments by the combined influence of climate, plants, animals (both those that live on and those that live in the soil), topography and time, measured in thousands of years. The processes involved – physical, chemical and biological – are generally grouped together under the term 'weathering'.

Physical processes include the breaking up of rocks through thermal expansion and contraction and abrasion by wind and water-borne solids. Chemical weathering requires water and oxygen, and involves the partial or complete dissolution of materials and the formation of others by the recombination of dissolved material. It is most rapid in the uppermost layers of a soil as these are generally warmer and contain more oxygen than lower layers. Living organisms, their activity and their generally acid secretions, have a marked effect on both the rate and the direction of weathering.

One way of understanding the complexity of weathering processes and the apparently vast variety of different soils formed is to group the processes under four headings:

- *Additions:* e.g. organic matter, which accumulates on the surface of the soil.
- *Removals:* e.g. soluble salts and carbonates leached to lower horizons.
- *Transfers:* e.g. of plant nutrients from lower horizons to the surface, or of soil material through the actions of animals such as earthworms.
- *Transformations:* e.g. weathering of primary minerals such as feldspar and biotite to silicate clay minerals and ions.

All these kinds of changes have been, and still are, operating in all soils but the balance among them varies from soil to soil depending on the chemical nature of the parent material, living organisms, topography, and, especially, climate.

Most soil types commonly occupy characteristic positions in a given landscape and may have a characteristic regional distribution. A simple example of this is the progression from a shallow, stony soil at the crest of a hill to deep alluvial loam or clay soil at the base of the slope. This is the principal reason for vines being planted half way up a hill so as to avoid the poor conditions at the top and the over-abundant water problem at the bottom.

Burgundian growers have the almost annual problem of returning 'wash-away' soil to their vineyards that has been washed to the bottom of the 'slopes' during rainy periods, while in the steeply sloped riverbank vineyards of Germany it is necessary to carry back the slate stones, washed down during the wet periods, that provide radiated warmth to the vines.

Soil Colour

The colour of a soil is determined mainly by the kinds and amounts of hydrated iron oxides present and the amount of organic matter it contains. There are several iron oxides, ranging in colour from yellow through orange and brown to red. Most soils contain mixtures of these oxides, with varying proportions giving the wide range of colours found. Black soils may derive their colour from organic matter or from specific minerals such as ilmenite.

Colour is a useful indicator of the aeration and drainage characteristics of soils, especially subsoils. The sequence from well aerated and well-drained to waterlogged is red-brown-yellow-mottled yellow-grey colours (grey, green-grey, black). The greenish-grey appearance of waterlogged soils is due to the presence of ferrous iron. If organic matter is present, black iron and manganese sulphides can be formed as well.

Organic matter darkens any soil, so that topsoils usually have a darker hue than subsoils. Soils that are light coloured or greyish in appearance have often been subjected to considerable leaching, probably because of the removal of coloured iron oxides.

Soil Texture

Soil particles range in size from gravel, through coarse and fine sand, to silt and clay. The proportions of these particles present in a soil, and especially its clay content, give the soil its typical 'feel' or texture.

Texture has an important bearing on the behaviour of soil in such operations as digging, cultivating and compacting, although soils of similar texture may react somewhat differently because of variations in the types of mineral particles. Soils are described as belonging to one of a number of texture grades between the extremes of pure clay and pure sand.

While the behaviour of soils with similar textures may be quite different, because of variations in the types of minerals present, the structural arrangement of these mineral particles, and the amount of organic matter present, it is still possible to make some general statements about the characteristics of soils of particular textures.

Water percolates readily through sands with little silt or clay; hence salts which might build up to high levels in heavier soils are readily leached from sands. On the other hand, fertilizers applied to sands are also readily leached out; special slow-release fertilizers are often used in sandy horticultural soils.

Much of our agricultural production comes from soils with friable loam surfaces. These soils contain moderate but variable amounts of all sizes of mineral particles together with organic matter. When at optimum moisture content they are readily cultivated for crops.

The properties of clay and clay soils – the so-called fine textured or fine grained soils – depend very much on the types of minerals present. Generally clay soils are difficult to cultivate unless self-mulching, being sticky when wet and setting hard when dry.

The structure of surface soils is determined, to a large extent, by their organic matter content. In addition, roots growing through the soil and the activity of micro-organisms produce pores and channels through which air and water can circulate and contribute to good structure. Both good structure and organic matter content increase under pressure. Large organic molecules from plant and animal residues adhering to the surfaces of clay minerals appear to contribute significantly to structure formation. Earthworms are particularly important in this regard.

Structure may be improved with heavy applications of organic matter, such as compost and animal manures, and for clay soils with high sodium content, by the addition of gypsum (calcium sulphate).

Soil Chemistry and Plant Growth

As well as providing a physical anchor for plants/vines, soils are also reservoirs for most of the chemical elements and water essential for plant growth. We saw earlier that fifteen mineral nutrients are necessary for healthy plants (see page 122). Others such as chromium, vanadium, nickel, selenium, iodine, fluorine, tin and silicon are not essential for plant growth but are taken up by them and so become available to animals, who need them for healthy growth.

All of these elements are accessible to plants through the breakdown of minerals and organic matter in the soil. The availability of the individual elements to the vine in a particular soil depends on:

(a) the amount present
(b) the forms in which it is present in the soil
(c) the rate at which it is released, and,
(d) the acidity or alkalinity of the soil; that is the much discussed pH.

Without labouring the business of soil or putting down those who shout loudest about its contribution to wine quality, let me say that the following paragraphs are of fundamental importance to anyone interested in yields from their own garden, whether it be flowers or fruit, or the variance in Chardonnay flavours from one vineyard to another.

Ions of the major nutrient elements potassium, calcium and magnesium (together with sodium) are held on the surfaces of negatively charged clay and humus particles, from where they may be taken up directly by plant roots or via the soil solution (water in which the plant nutrients are dissolved). An imbalance between the amounts of each of these ions can impair plant growth and will be reflected in fruit quality.

The availability of most elements is affected by changes in the soil's pH. As an example, heavy applications of lime may produce iron deficiency (lime chlorosis) and/or manganese deficiency, while acidifying a soil through the application of large amounts of fertilizers (such as ammonium sulphate and nitrate) may induce molybdenum deficiency or even manganese toxicity.

Plants need every one of the essential elements for growth. If just one is in short supply, growth will be poor despite the apparent abundance of all the others. Other than the reserves already in the soil, there are three main fertilizer sources – organic manures; crushed rocks, ores and minerals; and industrially produced fertilizers.

Before 1840, almost all fertilizers used were organic, consisting of farmyard manure, human excreta and plant materials of various kinds. We have come a long way since then, although I vividly recall the occupation of Japan in 1945 when only human excreta was used as fertilizer. On arising each morning one of my friends would inhale deeply and exclaim, 'Oh, for the pungent pong of poo!'

Soils and Water

When light rain falls most of it soaks down into the soil, travelling along cracks and channels and filling them up. If rain continues long enough the water penetrates further and further down until it reaches an impermeable layer (the so-called water table) – eventually becoming the water of springs, wells and bores. The texture, structure and porosity of a soil determine the rate at which water moves through it; penetration is rapid in sand but very slow into heavy clay.

Water in soils contains a wide range of organic and inorganic substances dissolved from soil organic matter and mineral particles; this is referred to as the 'soil solution'. Most of the nitrate, soluble sulphate and chloride ions in a soil are present in the soil solution which also contains low concentrations of ions of all the other essential nutrient elements needed by the vine. These ions are in dynamic equilibrium with others absorbed on to the surfaces of nearby clay mineral and organic particles. As vine roots remove nutrient ions from a soil, more ions move into the soil solution.

Vine roots are able to make contact with and absorb much of the water in a soil – but not all of it. In a waterlogged soil, oxygen used in microbiological activity is replaced too slowly for plant roots to be adequately supplied, so they soon die of asphyxiation.

For optimum growth, vine roots should explore as large a volume of soil for nutrients as possible. Light watering encourages only surface scavenging and leaves the vine, or plant, in a distressed situation during drought or periods without watering. However, the many reasons to graft vines on to rootstocks has caused much re-thinking about surface roots. This is discussed later.

Clones

When Raymond Bernard first arrived in Burgundy (he is now Délégué Régional, or Regional Director, at the Office National Interprofessionnel des Vins, Dijon) during the 1950s, he was distressed to see the condition of the Chardonnay vineyards. The queen of white varieties was seriously afflicted with degenerative diseases. The reduction in longevity of the vine, and numerous replantings of the same plot had successfully wrecked many of the vineyards. It was not uncommon for a vineyard to be pulled out after only twelve to fifteen years. The variety was being severely attacked by diseases that affected both yield and quality, and, when coupled with other vineyard blights such as *'coulure'* or *'millérandage'*, the structure and body of the wines were destroyed.

There was only one way out of the morass – find vines that were disease free (clonal selection, as it is known). This entails taking 'cuttings' from healthy 'mother' vines, thus a 'clone'. Each year, all possible cuttings are taken from the mother vine and successful progeny, a slow and tedious way to obtain millions of cuttings to replace the vineyards of Burgundy, where there are 10,000 vines planted to the hectare. Multiply that by Burgundy's 6,000 hectares of Chardonnay vines (today's figure) and the mammoth total is 60 million cuttings!

At this time, clonal selection research was proceeding apace in many countries such as Australia, California, Germany and Switzerland; and for many reasons. The principal ones were:

1. Increased productivity.
2. Improved quality – ability to produce fruit with lower pH, higher acid and sugar levels.
3. Better performance regarding the above in individual growing areas.
4. Virus diseases.
5. Compatibility with rootstocks and soils.

Australian researchers, and no doubt others, had determined that vine health automatically gave increased productivity and wine quality.

It was in 1955 that Burgundian researchers began 'clonal selection by cataloguing and identifying the mother vines with varying fruiting and growing potential'. As time went by, all this material was gathered together in a collection plot, that is to say in the same environment. So as to make lineal clonal comparisons more reliable all the material was grafted on a rootstock descended from the same mother vine, SO4. About 250 clones were gathered over several years, which allowed useful behavioural observations at different phenological stages, then the study of ripening development and finally, separate vintages and comparative vinifications.

Once the clones and rootstocks (see 'Rootstocks', pages 140) were happily married together by grafting, there began the monitoring of vine health in different areas of each state or *département*. This was followed by wine quality evaluation, taking into account seasonal climatic variations which can change both structure and flavour of the wines. This was, usually, conducted for each individual clone, the wine being made in small lots of ten to twenty litres.

Unfortunately, it is clear after thirty years of research that what is good in the way of clones or rootstocks for one country or region is not, necessarily, good for others. Examples of this would be the difference between Mâcon-Chablis-Champagne in France, New York-Napa Valley-Monterey in the USA and Mudgee-Mildura-Coonawarra in Australia; every region has its own individual needs in each of these countries. Annoyingly, this research work keeps a lot of people busy duplicating each other's work.

On the credit side, Burgundy's Chardonnay vineyards, while still undergoing some turmoil, have been restored to the stage where the vines' longevity has been doubled and yields increased from 29 hectolitres in 1960 to the 1980 figure of 70 hectolitres without any loss in wine quality. As yields from the same clone on different rootstocks can vary from 30–120 hectolitres per hectare (with considerable variation in quality), the correct matching of rootstocks and clones is vital for both fruit yield and wine quality.

This is the principal reason why most Burgundy vineyards are planted with several different clones of Chardonnay. Some clones have early budburst and ripen their fruit earlier, this is a real advantage in a cool, wet, slow ripening year. Other clones yield more fruit while still others provide better acid/sugar balance in the berries. A mixture of clones is now recommended in Burgundy.

The rigid European, French notably, appellation control laws prohibit the winemaker (legally) from sourcing fruit outside their own appellation, thereby limiting their choices. While the Burgundian grower is dependent on a multiplicity of clones and vineyards for flavour complexity, New World winemakers can draw fruit from any number of regions, or even other countries.

Pruning

The history of wine contains one fairy tale after another. Much is folklore, much is tradition; certainly, pruning fits into both categories. It is a simple fact that there is no one way to prune a vine. There is my way, your way, the *guyot* way – nearly as many methods as there are grapegrowers. One method is not to prune at all; that is after you have been through machine pruning (sawing, or hedging as it is known) and minimal pruning which entails a whip around the vineyard with a hedge cutter to whisk off a few low-lying canes that cannot be gathered up by the mechanical harvester. 'Nil' pruning is when these canes are 'tucked up' into the vine rather than severed.

Minimal Pruning of Cordon-trained Vines

The concept of minimal pruning of cordon-trained vines has its origins in the observation that sultana (Thompson's seedless) vines continue to produce large crops of acceptable fruit when left unpruned for a number of years. In this system, cordon-trained vines on a high single-vine wire are left unpruned but skirted below the wire to stop fruit and shoots from touching the ground.

Trials conducted in warm, irrigated Australian vineyards with sultana and a range of traditional and new winegrape varieties over ten seasons have shown that minimal pruning of cordon-trained vines can control shape and vigour and maintain or increase production. Traditional pruning not only appears to be un-necessary, but also leads to vigorous shoot growth. By contrast, cordon-trained vines have more but small shoots with fewer and closer nodes (the birthplace of leaves, tendrils, bunches and buds), and a smaller quantity of one-year-old wood.

For winegrape production, this system, in combination with mechanical harvesting, provides an effective system of manage-ment, reducing vigour, lowering costs and maximizing production of quality fruit. The system has been adopted commercially not only in warm, irrigated vineyards but also for vigorous vines in cool regions used for quality wine production.

If we start from the above statement, and set aside the emotions of tradition, we can consider the part pruning plays in wine quality.

Historically, the vine is not a self-supporting plant, but one that climbed trees towards the light. Even today, its long, fast-growing, flexible canes and tendrils attach themselves to trellis wires, or each other, for support. Long before the first century AD, grapegrowers all over the world were dabbling with pruning and trellising methods which we believe had their foundation in Egypt.

Reasons for Pruning

There are three traditional reasons for pruning:

1. Training – to ensure that each vine is developed to a regular shape appropriate to the space allotted in the vineyard.
2. Access – to ensure that the vineyard operations such as weed

control, irrigation, harvesting, pest and disease control can be performed smoothly and with minimum damage.

3. The primary aim of pruning is to regulate cropping in relation to the vigour of the vine.

   If pruning is too severe, the number of bunches developed will be small and, although these bunches and the berries may be large, the overall crop is usually reduced. The vine will respond by putting out watershoots (shoots arising from dormant buds in old wood) with excessive leaves creating dense shade and a humid environment conducive to disease.

If pruning is too light, a greater number of shoots will develop, bearing more bunches, which will, however, have fewer and smaller berries than normal. The crop may be larger in total, but quality, colour and maturity may be adversely affected. The ideal level of pruning is one which gives normal-sized, well-filled bunches of grapes, reaching maturity evenly and with well-balanced chemical composition, and at the usual time for that variety.

Another important aim is to position the fruiting area at the appropriate level to prevent shading out of parts of the vine and make harvesting as easy as possible. This is particularly important with mechanical harvesting.

The reason there are almost as many methods of pruning as there are vineyards, is quite simply that each viticultural district, regardless of size, has its own special needs due to soil types, water supply, geographical aspect or climate. In the end, the decision regarding pruning methods is a management one, with a healthy slice of tradition. It affects the cost of pruning, the cropping level, fruit quality (people such as brandy or bulk wine producers are seeking quantity rather than premium quality), and vine suitability for mechanical harvesting, where applicable.

In the non-cold areas of the New World, two hand-pruning methods – cane or spur – are popular. Briefly the difference is:

Spur pruning (Fig. 7) involves the reduction of the past season's canes to two bud spurs. During the following spring (pruning is done in the depths of winter) these buds will produce shoots that bear one, two or sometimes three bunches of grapes. To regulate the crop only a limited number of two bud spurs are left. These should be spaced evenly along the main arms of the vine. Spur pruning is relatively simple and less time-consuming than other methods.

Cane pruning (Fig. 8) is popular with premium grape growers.

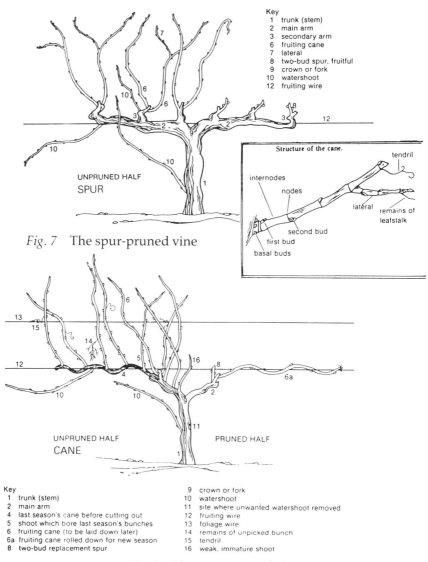

Key
1   trunk (stem)
2   main arm
3   secondary arm
6   fruiting cane
7   lateral
8   two-bud spur, fruitful
9   crown or fork
10   watershoot
12   fruiting wire

UNPRUNED HALF
SPUR

Structure of the cane.

internodes
nodes
second bud
first bud
basal buds

tendril
lateral
remains of
leafstalk

Fig. 7   The spur-pruned vine

UNPRUNED HALF
CANE

PRUNED HALF

Key
1   trunk (stem)
2   main arm
4   last season's cane before cutting out
5   shoot which bore last season's bunches
6   fruiting cane (to be laid down later)
6a   fruiting cane rolled down for new season
8   two-bud replacement spur

9   crown or fork
10   watershoot
11   site where unwanted watershoot removed
12   fruiting wire
13   foliage wire
14   remains of unpicked bunch
15   tendril
16   weak, immature shoot

Fig. 8   The cane-pruned vine

With this method, selected canes are supported, by wrapping along the trellis wire, at the desired fruiting height. The number of canes depends on the vine's vigour, as with spur pruning the cropping level is partly determined by the number of fruitful buds (nodes) retained. The ever-escalating cost of cane pruning is causing many vinegrowers to change from this method to either spur or mechanical pruning.

In areas dependent solely on rainfall, somewhere between forty to sixty buds per vine are left at pruning, as this number, in a normal season, will provide a good quality crop. With supplementary irrigation, where a regular yield and crop can be more easily attained, the number of buds may be doubled.

Mechanical pruning

Many growers world-wide now use this method regularly due to enormous cost savings, as much as 75 per cent in some cases. The vines are either 'square' sawn and left, or are sawn and then hand finished in two ways:

1. At walking pace, pickers cut any obvious canes missed by the machines.
2. More care in cutting vines back to the two-bud system. This system can provide large savings.

In cold regions – those with minimal sunshine hours such as parts of Canada, Champagne and Chablis – shaping and trellising vines takes on a more important role so that the foliage canopy is opened up and the fruit obtains maximum exposure to the sun. Developments such as the Geneva double curtain system have made it possible to grow noble varieties in areas that were unsuitable prior to the development of such trellising methods, and this has brought good wine closer to more people.

As the vine leaf is a sun-generated sugar-producing factory for the berry, it is vital, in regions with limited sun hours, to have sufficient leaf area to cater for this operation known as photosynthesis. Cool area grapes may ripen earlier than those hot regions, as excessive heat can cause the vine to 'shut down'. Cool areas can have problems ripening fruit before the season breaks. In European years of insufficient sunshine, winemakers are allowed to chaptalize (increase the sugar level) the wine by adding beet sugar to bring it up to the minimum legal level.

The Fruit

Grape bunches are classified into various shapes – shouldered, winged, conical and cylindrical. Chardonnay is a shouldered variety; the berries are spherical and, when ripe, are a transparent green-gold colour.

Like much other fruit, the green berry is high in acid and contains almost no sugar. A green apple is a typical example of acid tartness. Following *véraison* (the start of the ripening process when the berry changes from its all-green colour), the sugar level starts to rise and the acid level commences its decline. It is the length of time, inspired by the vine's micro- and macroclimate, between *véraison* and ultimate ripeness, that will dictate the fruit quality and much of the flavour of the resulting wine. A good analogy is that of cooking meat: too much heat too quickly will yield a tough and dry roast. A lower, more even heat will produce a tender, juicy delicacy.

The essential difference between the so-called 'flinty' and 'steely' wines of Chablis/Burgundy and the rich, full-flavoured 'block-busters' of the New World, is the ability of the macroclimate fully to ripen the fruit. (Although in most cases, the New World wine-makers have moved away from the now-unfashionable oak/fruit blockbuster styles of the 1970s.)

In climates where wines are struggling to reach 12 per cent by volume of alcohol (naturally), it is normal for acid levels to be high, and viscosity low, thus giving the 'steely' connotation. These matters are discussed more fully in Part Four, Making Chardonnay.

Vine Stress

Yet another time-worn fairytale is the 'vine stress' theory, a belief that the more the vine is stressed the better the resulting wine quality. This notion is about 10 per cent true.

There are a number of ways a vine can be stressed, and most have a deleterious effect. For a vine to function normally it must be in balance, just like our own body. Whether it is temperature stress – heat/cold; water stress – too much/too little; or wind or nutritional stress, the vine will be thrown out of balance, its feeding routine upset, which in turn will change the chemical composition of the grape and its ultimate quality and flavour. These climatic variations are responsible for the so-called 'good' and 'bad' vintages.

Climate

Climate is the one major factor over which the winegrower has no control. A 'good' year is one of ideal or almost ideal climatic conditions, but as a destructive force causing 'bad' years, the climate, generally, or any of its elements, can be a factor at any time of the year. These are:

TEMPERATURE
Too cold   – can kill the vine
Frost   – just like a fire, frost will burn-off the baby buds causing heavy crop losses. Having early bud-burst, Chardonnay is particularly prone to frost damage.
Too hot   – water stress to vines, low acid levels, high pH, cooked/burnt fruit.
RAIN
Too much – at flowering: will reduce the number of berries per bunch
         – during the growing year necessitates costly spray programmes to eliminate rot and mildew. At harvest time causes fruit splitting and rotting, lower sugar and acid levels.
Too little – Small shoots, low leaf area and insufficient sugar production.
HAIL
In short, a disaster at any time, not only causing fruit damage to the current year's crop but, by damaging buds, can dramatically affect the following year's crop.
HUMIDITY
Humidity is the catalyst for several unwanted diseases. *Pourriture grise* or grey rot forms on the berries. This mould is also known as botrytis cinerea or 'noble rot' and is famous for the part it plays in the flavour of luscious sweet table wines made from Sauvignon (blanc) and Riesling. It is an unwelcome visitor to Chardonnay vineyards as it makes constant and costly spraying necessary.
Oïdium, which grows on the surface of the vine, also causes the Chardonnay grower to spray often for protection.

While the world has many varying climates, there are three main types known, viticulturally, as temperate, Mediterranean and continental. The *temperate* climates are those having mainly summer rains and high humidity, such as the eastern USA, eastern Australia north of Sydney, much of France, South America and China. *Mediterranean* climates enjoy dry summers, with rainfall in winter and spring. These areas are, as the name suggests, along the Mediterranean shores, the west coast of the USA, much of southern Australia and all of the New Zealand viticultural areas. A *continental* climate is typified by those inland areas like Champagne and Burgundy that have very cold winters and hot summers.

A grower in a Mediterranean type region may spray for humidity provoked diseases three or four times annually, where as the temperate climate grower may have to spray as many as fifteen times each season; a very expensive difference.

Heat Summation

For further understanding of climate and geography, we will now turn to the subject of heat summation – the standard technique used in comparing the almost infinite permutations of climatic and geographical features that make up any wine appellation. Basically, it is a way of measuring one of the most critical elements of viticulture – the amount of heat involved in the growing and ripening processes of the fruit.

Vines do not like being too close to the Equator or Poles. Other than these obvious questions of latitude, there are three major factors affecting the amount of heat provided to the vines: water, soil and elevation.

Water
Many of the historical regions are on slopes close to large bodies of water which store heat during the day and release it at night, thus giving the area around the vines – the microclimate – a desirable evenness of temperature. One thinks of Germany's Rhine Valley, France's Valley of the Marne, or of Bordeaux, between the Atlantic Ocean and the Gironde River.

Winegrowers around the Finger Lakes of New York State and the regions in Ohio and New York bordering Lake Erie, are very conscious of the impact of these large water bodies in equalizing temperatures. Many of the new viticultural areas of the world – Long Island, New York; New Zealand and Margaret River, Western Australia, all enjoy the benefit of large oceans on their doorstep.

Soil
A second factor affecting the vines' microclimate is stoney soil, which, like water bodies, stores heat during the day and

thus contributes to diurnal evenness between day and night temperatures.

Elevation

The third factor is elevation. Obviously, the higher we go above sea level, the cooler the climate. It is only the 997 metres elevation of Lubbock in the Texas 'panhandle' that makes the growing of Chardonnay possible in this 34°N latitude. The slopes of Burgundy and the coastal ranges of California are both examples of high vineyards.

To complete the vine's cycle, it should become dormant during winter. After this sleep, vines come to life with the first flush of spring when the temperature reaches about 10°C (50°F). Depending on the heat summation, Chardonnay will ripen anywhere between 150 to 220 days from budburst. The one sin of Chardonnay is its penchant for bursting forth on the first few warm days of spring. Should this be followed by a frost, the new growth will be burnt off and the season ruined before it starts. For this reason Chardonnay cannot be grown in any region without a reliable 150 days frost-free span.

Vineyard Siting

To help with site selection, researchers at the University of California, Davis, some years ago developed the *degree days*, or heat summation, technique. The heat summation is arrived at by totalling the number of degrees above a mean of 10°C for each day of the growing season. In the northern hemisphere this is from 1 April to 30 October and in the southern hemisphere from 1 October to 30 April. By way of example, if we take the total temperature for the 30 days of April as 509°C, then deduct 10° for each of the 30 days, we have a monthly heat summation of 209. These heat units are added for each day of the growing season to arrive at the heat summation. Grapes need a minimum of 945 such units to have any chance of ripening, and above 2,900 they are not even any use for curry.

The viticultural areas of the world have been divided into five regions of heat summation; North America and Australia are represented in all five. Regions one and two are ideally suited to dry white table wines of distinction, as the fruit ripens late in the season allowing maximum flavour build up. In the warmer region three, fruit fully ripens earlier providing wines with more body/viscosity. Grapes that mature quickly produce wines suitable for drinking at a young age; these wines come from the warmer regions, four and five.

All this is a generalization, as the most expensive sweet table wines come from regions one and two and some splendid and expensive Chardonnays come from regions four and five.

Rootstocks

If we are interested in why Chardonnay tastes differently from one vineyard/winery to another, we must learn – to coin a phrase – from the roots up. As we have seen in the preceding pages, wine is made in the vineyard. The soil is an anchor, with the soil solution and the micro- and macroclimates all playing their parts in providing the root system with essential nutrients.

The idea of rootstocks came about through the introduction to France of a root-sucking louse, named phylloxera, in the 1860s. Very soon, it had chomped its way through the mighty, and not so mighty, vineyards of Europe and the rest of the world – wherever *vinifera* vines were grown. Great vineyards were reduced to nothing better than cow paddocks. This little pest from the Mississippi Valley had the viticultural world on its knees. It also showed to what absurd lengths politicians, universally, will go in the face of rural disaster. Around the world, crazy legislation went on the statute books, and for two decades the scientific world was beaten by this pest – just as it is today by AIDS and the common cold.

While most American native vines have few problems with phylloxera, the brutal truth is that their fruit makes lousy wine and could not be sustained for that purpose. As with so many of life's disasters, the remedy eventually came from a simple compromise – grafting the non-resistant scions/vines to the resistant American roots – hence rootstocks. Even today, more than a century later, the matching of rootstocks and scions is still being fine-tuned in almost every viticultural area of the world, due mainly to the breeding of superior clones.

Just as one particular clone will perform admirably in a given region and poorly in a neighbouring one, rootstocks have specific rather than general applications.

Rootstocks have three basic origins:

1. Native American Vines: *Vitis rupestris* and *Vitis riparia*
2. An American native vine crossed (X) with another American

native wild vine: *Vitis rupestris* × *Vitis riparia* or *berlandieri* × *rupestris* and other hybrid crosses.
3. American native vine × European *vinifera*.

Ever since the earliest days, vine breeders in many countries have continued crossing the American natives with hybrids of these vines, and hybrids of the hybrids of the hybrids. These 'backroom boys' have, through diligence and application, produced one miracle after another. It is quite dedicated work, and as a reward might have a vine named for them! We all benefit in our glass of wine.

The original use for rootstocks was to make the *vinifera* vines completely resistant to phylloxera. In Australia and the USA, some areas were not affected by the pest and many vineyards in these regions preferred not to use phylloxera-resistant rootstocks, or any rootstocks at all. Even though there are quarantine restrictions against the import of vine canes or rootlings into a number of states in the New World, sadly these laws are flouted and phylloxera is rearing its ugly head again in too many places. In fact, phylloxera exists in all winegrowing countries with the exception of Australia's western Victoria, and South and Western Australia.

Since the early days of rootstocks, plant breeders have realized the potential of these 'surrogate mothers' and have developed rootstocks to overcome many other soil and disease problems, such as excessive salinity, lime, acid, infertility, clay, overly rich soils, and nematodes (worms). These rootstocks can be either phylloxera *resistant* or *tolerant* of the disease. But while they might be marvellous in, say, salty soils, they will give no guarantee against the dreaded louse. A nematode trial being conducted in South Australia gives some idea of rootstocks' true value. 1.B.10.1 clonal canes grown on their own roots produced 2 kilograms fruit per vine. The same clonal material grown on Ramsay rootstocks yielded 15 kilograms.

Prior to grafting, there is a perfect relationship between all parts of the vine – the roots, leaves and fruit. Affinity of rootstock and scion means retaining this anatomical and physiological harmony when a *vinifera* vine is grafted on to an American or hybrid rootstock. The physiological functions of vines vary enormously, more so when put under the stress of grafting.

The grapegrower is almost in a no-win situation: phylloxera thrives in clay soils and worms just love sandy soils. The nematode pest presents a multiple problem in that it comes in three forms requiring, in many cases, different rootstocks for each problem.

However, things are not all bad for growers who carefully tend their vines and vineyards. Science is making great strides with disinfectants and soil sprays, and better rootstocks are being applied to soils we understand more each day.

Harvest Time

The harvest (or *vendange* in French) is a nervous time for the vinegrowers, when to pick or not to pick is the (very expensive) question. In cool climates, where the season can break at any time, the skies may open and down will come the ruinous rain in bucketsful. The grower is anxious to get the grapes into the winery and the money into the bank. The grapegrower can grow but one crop each year and this is the business end of a year's work. The winemaker wants the grapes at the peak of condition, the best possible chemical composition, acid and pH, plus the maximum amount of varietal flavour in the berries for his particular needs.

But what is ripe? A laconic contribution came from one California grapegrower who said ripeness was when the winemaker said 'Pick them!' It is here that the Chardonnay grape is different from most others; the Champagne and table winemaker have entirely different specifications. The makers of bubbly do not want the ripe varietal characters sought by the conventional winemaker, rather a lean wine with crisp acidity to achieve the relatively light-bodied style of Champagne.

About three weeks before the suggested harvest date, the wine-maker and the grower will start their vigil taking regular samples from all over the vineyard. There are almost as many methods of testing as there are vineyards, but a popular one is the 200 berry selection from bunches, both shaded and unshaded, from the top and bottom of bunches scattered throughout the vineyard. Above all, the sample must be a representative one. What constitutes an ideal grape chemical composition for making Chardonnay is as personal as one's choice of a partner; nearly everyone has a different set of criteria.

It is not hard to see that the parameters are very wide. They would rarely range this amount in one given region, but world-class Chardonnays can and are made with these variations. If you think this is hard to believe, be prepared for an enormous surprise when it comes to methodology.

In Europe, it is not unusual for the mayor of the town, aided by advice from the local Comité, to make a formal announcement that it is time to gather the harvest. The harvest dates in Champagne and Burgundy, as a rule, fall between the last week of September and the first week of October, a span of something like fourteen days. These dates are very similar in California.

However, things are very different in the southern hemisphere (six months earlier) where the harvest can commence during the first week of February and finish in early May, a time span of ninety days. Little wonder that the styles are different! If we take a look at the Chardonnay growing season from budburst to harvest, the general run of cool northern hemisphere vineyards, on either side of the Atlantic, occupies 175 days, whereas in the bottom half of the world in the cool growing areas of Coonawarra, South Australia and Marlborough, New Zealand, it covers periods of up to 227 days. This extended growing season produces fruit of outstanding quality.

Machines or Humans?

Having determined that the fruit is ripe and that the winery is ready to receive it, the next decision is whether to harvest by hand or machine. This is another emotive and long debated issue. The essential difference between the two methods is that *machines pick berries, humans pick bunches*. The close spacing of vines in European vineyards has caused some problems in developing machines that are able to work in those confines; this has now been overcome. However, the Champagne appellation laws forbid the use of mechanical harvesters as the grapes must be pressed as whole bunches. Also, in most Champagne vineyards, each bunch is checked in the vineyard for faulty berries before transportation to the winery.

Not so as we proceed south through Burgundy, where machines are becoming a popular sight in the vineyards and towns, especially among the progressive commercial 'shipper' vineyards. Yet, mechanically harvested fruit still represents only the tip of the iceberg and the traditional end-of-vintage happy pickers' parties will remain a feature of French viticulture for many a year.

It is a different story in the vast vineyards of the New World, with wide-row spacing that enables the giant mechanical harvesters to pick up to 140 tonnes in a twenty-hour day. While the inland irrigated projects are almost exclusively machine harvested, for a variety of reasons, only about 50 per cent of other areas use machines. The most common reason is the belief that hand-picked fruit is less damaged. In Australia, the figure would be more like

80 per cent mechanical harvesting, while in the USA most Chardonnay is hand-picked.

Small vineyard holdings are normally hand-picked as are many vineyards within a kilometre or two of the processing facility. While the majority of machine-picked fruit will also come from vineyards in similar areas, a lot of New World vineyards may be located hundreds of kilometres away in isolated regions.

Advocates of machine-harvesting list these advantages:

1. *Machines can harvest in the cool of the night*; many start at midnight, making it possible to deliver fruit in better condition than if picked in the heat of the day.
2. *Speed*; if weather threatens, machines can quickly gather the fruit. Also, at this hottest time of the year, speed helps bring in fruit at optimum ripeness. A machine can work twenty effective hours per day for seven days each week.
3. *Cost efficiency*; using Australian figures (which are, possibly, representative) in dry farmed, broadacre vineyards a machine can cover half a hectare in one hour at an hourly cost of $170. Taking as an example a 15 tonne/hectare crop the machine would, in eight hours, harvest 4 hectares or 60 tonnes. Human pickers on wages are estimated to pick one half tonne per eight-hour day, thus, 120 pickers to do the same job. These would work in gangs of eight people and would require three tractors and trailers, three drivers, three bucket handlers and a minimum of 5,000 buckets.

PART FOUR
Making Chardonnay

The Winery

At long last, the grapes have survived the fury of nature and are ready to be taken to the finishing school. Here the fruit will be either enhanced and converted into a masterpiece, damned to mediocrity, or even worse, destroyed beyond all recognition. Great wines cannot be made from poor fruit, but poor wines can easily be made from great fruit.

However, I believe that the quality of the finished wine should be able to be predicted from the quality of the fruit prior to fermentation. I am also firmly of the opinion that wherever good grapes can be grown, great wines can be made. In both cases, when all things are equal, the ultimate quality of the wine rests squarely on the skill and philosophy of the winemaker. Any number of outstanding wines are consistently made in Texas, New York, Canada, New Zealand, Western Australia or wherever, while nextdoor neighbours languish in mediocrity. The major reason is adherence to the 'If it was good enough for my father . . .' philosophy, coupled with outdated and poor winemaking practices.

Earlier, I said that Chardonnay was the artist's full palette. While there are some Rieslings made with oak cask treatment and Cabernets without said oak, Chardonnay offers the opportunity to 'oak or not to oak' in equal proportions, plus about 200 other variations. For this reason alone, I think it is appropriate to recount an interview with California oenologist, Bob Mueller:

As for being definite on Chardonnay, to be perfectly honest, I don't feel that I know what the end product is, or really, how to define it. Or, in fact, that we know all the answers right now. I think we are learning more as we go along; we are breaking apart the things we think make the difference: malolactic fermentation or no, stirring [*bâtonnage*], racking with and without aeration, and so on. We are trying to find out and decide for ourselves what is making the difference. I must say that we are not necessarily there yet . . . Maybe they [the Burgundians] are like us: they don't understand all the differences or how it happens, that it works successfully and that they are happy with it. But I think the world at large is trying to understand Chardonnay more and what they can do to get more out of it. There are so many things – new barrels, old barrels, clones and sites – that go into Chardonnay; it is almost endless. I think we must admit that we don't yet understand everything about Chardonnay.

In winemaking, at least, cleanliness comes before godliness. Any winery building, its machinery, equipment, corks, bottles and people, are all sources of possible bacterial infection, and the air we breathe is for ever wanting to help destroy the vinegrowers' annual efforts. Because of the robustness that red wines draw from phenolics in the grape skins, they are not quite so prone to the damaging effects of oxidation. With wine, like any new baby, it is difficult to be too careful. Chardonnay, the most robust of white table wine varieties, can also benefit from some of those phenolics. Oxygen *per se* is not all bad; as long as it is controlled it can be beneficial.

Let us now look at how Chardonnay wine can be made and at how all the variables are used to enhance and alter the flavour of the finished product. The major steps in Chardonnay production are: harvesting, crushing, draining, pressing, clarifying, adjustments, yeast inoculation, primary fermentation, malolactic fermentation and barrels.

Crushing and Destemming

When the grapes arrive at the winery the winemaker has the choice of crushing – with or without stems – or pressing the whole bunch. Crushing and pressing are not good terms as the grapes are treated rather gently, sufficient to break the skins and certainly not to crush them in the literal sense. This would break the seeds and extract extreme bitterness from both the seeds and stems.

The major benefit of treating whole bunches allows the free-run juice better movement through the mass of pulp and skins. Many makers like to beat the berries from the stems and treat berries only.

At this time the winemaker decides whether or not to have skin contact (maceration) of juice and skins. This is a much debated decision. The proponents of maceration say it gives body, colour and flavour, while those opposed say it gives bitterness and none of the above. The Burgundians do not believe in skin contact at all.

Sulphur dioxide (SO_2) is another contentious issue at this stage. It has been in use for 2,000 years for anti-oxygen and anti-microbial purposes. While the very large producers of low-middle priced wines would use SO_2 at the crusher, makers of the more specialized barrel-fermented wines are evenly split as to the use of SO_2 prior to fermentation. The Bugundians do; many New World makers do not.

Some winemakers believe that the early addition of SO_2 adds to the wine's bouquet; frankly I see it as a flavour minus. During the international judgements in Beaune and London it was terribly easy to identify the newcomers to Chardonnay making by the amounts of SO_2 used, thoroughly spoiling the wines. Sulphur dioxide is expressed as free (active), bound (inactive) or total. It is the free sulphur that provides the protection.

The free-run juice is held in a settling tank and fractions of the pressed wine are added, the amount is an individual decision. Sometimes no press juice is added. This allows the solids in the wine to settle to the bottom of the container and the clean juice is moved from these gross lees. Most winemakers prefer to have a large proportion of the solids filtered out as they can be the source of unpleasant flavours. Some winemakers prefer to leave a portion as they provide food for the yeast and 'character', if that can be defined. It certainly can be described in some badly made wines!

Primary Fermentation

The miracle of fermentation turns grape juice into wine. Yeast enzymes convert the grape sugars into approximately equal parts of alcohol and carbon dioxide (CO_2). The amount of alcohol in the finished wine can be accurately predicted by the amount of sugar in the grapes at harvest time. Grape sugar is measured in degrees *brix* or, depending on the country, degrees *Baumé*. One degree *Baumé* equals 1.8 per cent sugar in the grape juice, whereas one degree *brix* equals .9 per cent. One degree *Baumé* before fermentation is approximately 1 per cent of alcohol by volume when fermentation is completed. Grapes picked at 10° *Baumé* will produce a wine of approximately 10 per cent of alcohol by volume.

Yeast Selection

Here again, the maker's choice of yeast may be as important in the final wine flavour as the region or *terroir* from which the grapes originate, or the barrels used for fermentation and/or maturation. As a general rule, the New World winemaker will use a cultured or dry yeast, whereas his Burgundian counterpart will use the natural yeast that is resident on the bloom of the grape berry.

During 1986, California's *Practical Winery* magazine conducted an in-depth survey of Chardonnay winemaking techniques and practices across the USA, and the results from 200 winemakers were reported in the November/December 1986 issue. In the survey, the most popular yeasts in use were: Champagne, Montrachet, Eperney 11, Prise de Mousse and Chanson. Champagne and Montrachet together accounted for 50 per cent of the respondents' preferred yeast. It can be seen that most of the preferred yeasts come from Champagne or Burgundy. Wild yeasts in the New World vineyards are generally unreliable and can do weird things to wine. One of the reasons for adding SO_2 before fermentation is to kill or inhibit the natural wild yeasts on the grape bloom.

Almost without exception, New World winemakers are content to inhibit the wild yeasts and inoculate the Chardonnay juice with known yeast cultures. The choice of the yeast, particularly when no sulphur is used prior to fermentation, is critical for two important reasons. First, the introduced yeast must be active and numerous enough to dominate the fermentation, and second, the strain must introduce no bad side effects, something that often happens. It could be said that some winemakers choose a yeast for what it will *not* do rather than what it will do, the introduction of hydrogen sulphide (H_2S), for example, which gives a smell of rotten eggs; not a favoured flavour in Chardonnay!

Yeast comes in two different forms, the pre-prepared dried form and an active culture on an agar slope from a laboratory. Like wine or beer (two products of yeast fermentation) yeasts come in many brands, flavours and uses. The selection is normally based on local performance as opposed to their overseas reputation. As the flavour of the finished wine is almost 'set in stone' during the fermentation, the choice of the right yeast is paramount. Some of the criteria that are important in the selection of a yeast are:

1. Alcohol tolerance – some yeasts are killed as the alcohol level increases.
2. Sugar/alcohol yield.
3. Ester and higher alcohol production (i.e. aroma impact).
4. The production of volatile acidity, acetaldehyde and pyruvate.
5. Fermentation speed and tendency to produce foam.
6. Adaption for re-starting 'stuck' fermentations.
7. Relationship to the killer factor – or presence of the killer factor.
8. Optimum temperatures – and temperature sensitivity.

Rather than expand on each of the criteria above, let microbiologist Dr Paul Monk relate what happens in a typical fermentation:

When you take control of the fermentation by inoculating with a selected yeast strain, you are going to get certain responses. The response to that strain is very much dependent on the composition of the must, as the yeast can only grow in the environment it seeks. If you take the same yeast strain and vary the temperature of the fermentation, you will vary the balance of the end products formed by this one yeast. With strain 729, if you ferment at 20°C it's ok, but ferment at 10°C and you'll get two grams per litre of acetic acid. (An acceptable standard is 0.7 grams.) Some people like higher levels and some wines, particularly sweet ones can carry more acetate. You'll find that the results of the yeast, in terms of the aroma of the wine, will depend on how the winemaker handles it. Extremes of temperature, anaerobic conditions and CO_2 'blanketing' of the must may produce great big faults, even with good quality fruit.

The function of the yeast is to get into that juice and get out as quickly as possible so that the winemaker can get on with the business of making his wine. The real contribution is from the quality of the grapes, and the handling, blending and maturing of the wine after it is made. However, if that fermentation, which is a very important aspect of it, is fraught with problems and difficulties, then you will not make great wine. For example, if you start off with a low temperature fermentation rather than using temperature control to raise the fermentation you'll vary the end products, and may even have a 'stuck' fermentation. The handling of the fermentation is important, and so is the composition of the must.

There is a trend today to select vigorous strains that are fairly neutral. Careful attention is then given to promote a large population of healthy yeast cells that will complete the fermentation at a steady rate with minimal unfavourable by-products.

As the Canadian yeast specialist, Clayton Cone, told me: 'All of the accolades surrounding Chardonnay, such as noble, fat, fleshy, bold, warm, jovial, generous, fruity, crisp, firm and so on all have to be due to the quality of the grape and to the cellar practices. Some of those negative sensory evaluations can be related to poor fermentation practices.'

If anything is central to this whole work it is the preceding few paragraphs. The ultimate good and bad flavours of Chardonnay, or any other wine for that matter, revolve around fermentation and cellar practices. Assuming that the winemaker starts with good fruit, it is here that the true varietal flavours are enhanced or destroyed. No amount of oak, new or otherwise, can replace the true flavour of fruit.

The two most common yeast types are *Saccharomyces bayanus* (SB) and *Saccharomyces cerevisiae* (SC). Each has a particular use, either for red or white wines. A different strain will, more than likely, be used for sweet or sparkling wines. The popular strains in the USA, as mentioned are: Champagne (SC), Montrachet (SC), Epernay 11 (SC), Prise de Mousse (SC) and Chanson (SC).

For several decades the Australian Wine Research Institute has been extremely active in yeast research and development and many Australian winemakers have participated in these developments. For this reason, there is possibly a larger selection of yeasts used in Australia than in any other country and it could be said that there is no popular, or common yeast strain – wet or dry. It is a different story in New Zealand where Prise de Mousse is a popular favourite.

As Clayton Cone suggested to me, rightly or wrongly, winemakers *perceive* different aroma characters in each different yeast strain. One splendid example of this is winemaker Richard Arrowood who uses a mixture of yeasts for specific tasks. For the McRae Vineyard in Sonoma he uses the Montrachet yeast to modify the intense flavour of the grapes. This yeast is also used when requiring more richness in a particular wine. The Montrachet yeast needs careful handling, as H_2S can be a monstrous side effect. However, a Champagne yeast is used for fruit from the Robert Young, Alexander Valley Vineyards. He finds it necessary to ferment these two yeasts at quite different temperatures. Like many winemakers in the New World, Arrowood also uses a mixture of yeasts in one particular wine to obtain more complex aroma characters.

The Ferment

After the must has settled, the winemaker then has another decision of importance, a stylistic one made well in advance: whether to ferment in stainless steel tanks, oak casks or both. This is what happens.

When stainless steel tanks are used the must is inoculated in the tanks and fermentation is allowed to continue until all the sugar is converted to alcohol. A 'stuck' fermentation is when the yeast dies or stops working before completion. This normally happens through lack of yeast 'food', such as nitrogen, vitamins and amino acids. Excessive alcohol or very hot temperatures will cause the fermentation to stick, leaving the unfinished wine a 'sitting duck' for bacterial spoilage due to the remaining unfermented sugar.

In the case of barrel fermentation, the must is pumped into casks, the choice of new or old oak – and the degree of 'toasting' or 'charring' – is a stylistic and economic one. Wines that are made in new oak are generally the most expensive, regardless of their origin. The standard practice in Burgundy is to use old barrels, but an increasing number are using new wood. As the fermentation proceeds, the wine becomes frothy and looks as though it is boiling. Because the wine foams as it ferments, the barrels can only be filled to 75–80 per cent capacity. A fermentation 'trap' inserted in the bung hole allows the CO_2 to escape without letting oxygen in. Filling the barrels so that none of the wine is lost, and, at the same time, not allowing space for sufficient oxygen to spoil the wine, is a tricky business.

At the completion of fermentation in either vessel, another key set of philosophical and stylistic decisions is made. In the case of the stainless steel made wine, is it to be given oak barrel ageing or not, and if so, how long? Also, should the wine be filtered and sent to the oak 'clean as a whistle', or with some light lees? For the barrel fermented wines (now that fermentation is over, must has become wine) the decisions are:

1. Leave as is, no filtering, racking or movement – this is the most practised style in Burgundy and is becoming popular among what are regarded as the top-priced producers in the New World. This is known as the '*sur-lies*' method.
2. Rack off lees.
3. Filter off lees. (Both 2 and 3 would normally go into new barrels for maturation.)

For the benefit of overview, I will rely heavily on the excellent Chardonnay survey conducted by *Practical Winery*. This survey had an exceptionally large sampling and expresses the situation in the New World generally. It showed about an equal split between fermentations in oak barrels and stainless steel, with 50 out of 200 respondents using both.

As mentioned in the survey, about 25 per cent of producers in the New World use both barrel and stainless steel fermentations. This can be achieved by blending finished portions of each method, or by starting the fermentation in stainless steel and then (at a time of the winemaker's own choosing) placing all, or a portion of, the wine into oak casks to complete it. As a rule of thumb, the price of a bottle of Chardonnay can be linked to the amount of fermentation and maturation time the wine has spent in new oak during these two stages. Not only is new oak very expensive, but the processing time is lengthy, labour intensive and fraught with numerous risks.

At this stage it is important to point out that there is no such thing as a 'typical' Burgundian winemaking method. In quantity, there is probably more white Burgundy made in stainless steel than in oak casks, but there is little doubt that a great number of producers use casks. The bottom of the range products from the large négociants might see some oak on their way through the winery, but oak is not part of the style. However, these same négociants are responsible for many of the finest wines made by the '*sur-lies*' method, as are many small producers in Meursault, Montrachet, Mâcon and the Pouilly-Fuissé regions.

Malolactic Fermentation

As the reader may have already noted, there are many contentious issues involved in making Chardonnay; none more so than malolactic fermentation (MLF). In France, whether it be Champagne,

Chablis or Burgundy, there is no problem; it happens, everyone does it, like it or not. Nature takes care of that! But it is a very different story in the New World. In the *Practical Winery* survey, winemakers were split almost evenly on the concept of the MLF for Chardonnay, 46 per cent encouraging it and 54 per cent avoiding it. The MLF is used more on higher priced wines and in cooler regions. Of those who encourage the MLF, slightly more than one-third complete it, while the other two-thirds achieve only partial completion. Eighty-two per cent inoculate with a commercial strain of bacteria; just over 17 per cent allowing spontaneous fermentation.

Grapes, as opposed to wine, have numerous acids, the main pair being malic and tartaric. Malic acid is the harsh acid that gives a green apple its bite. Grapes grown in cold climates are normally higher in malic acid and it is desirable that a portion of the total amount is converted to the much softer lactic acid. Unlike the primary fermentation, lactic acid bacteria, rather than yeast, is responsible for the MLF. This group of bacteria – Lactobacillus, Leuconostic, and Pediococcus – plays a key role in the preparation of fermented milk products such as butter, cheese and yoghurt, as well as pickles, Sauerkraut and sausage! The odour of cheese and butter is favourably associated with Chardonnay and derives from an MLF by-product – diacetyl – a chemical used to give margarine its butter-like smell. Diacetyl is also a component of hazelnuts and is possibly the source of the oft-used hazelnut/roasted hazelnut descriptor so commonly associated with white Burgundy and old Champagne.

Another by-product – acetic acid – is mainly a negative odour in Chardonnay and is often detected as a pickle or Sauerkraut odour.

The normal effects of MLF are:

1. Reduction in acidity and an increase in pH. This makes the MLF an advantage in cold climates where the grapes have high acidity and de-acidification is a real problem. It is a minus in warm areas where acid levels are usually low. In bad years, such as 1981 and 1984 to a lesser degree, the reduction of acidity in unripe grapes is a real problem in Burgundy.
2. Increased microbiological stability, mainly avoiding the MLF happening in the bottle. Unfortunately, the MLF also produces CO_2, or bubbles, and should it take place in the bottle, buyer beware!
3. Modified flavour by creating minute traces of several volatile compounds that heighten the sensory value of the wine and

also add to the mouth-feel and viscosity. These include ethyl acetate, diacetyl, glycerine, acetoin and acetic acid.

Internationally the wine industry is still learning about MLF, a situation that makes for many hypotheses as to when the MLF should start. There is general agreement in the New World that the timing is critical. In France there is no such problem because the MLF happens after the completion of the primary fermentation, just as night follows day, even if the primary fermentation is in autumn and the MLF in spring.

The majority opinion in the New World is for the MLF to be inoculated after the PF while another smaller group believes that both the PF and the MLF should be undertaken together; each has his own valid argument. These are of a highly technical nature. It is believed that the natural bacteria on French grapes, in fact, do start their work during PF and conclude it immediately thereafter, unless inhibited by the onset of cold weather in which case nothing happens until cellar temperatures warm up in the spring. For this reason, an increasing number of Burgundy cellars are being heated.

However, both fermentations do not happen together: because of high volatile acidity problems (which gives a vinegary smell to wine) Burgundians avoid the double fermentation like the plague.

Ideal conditions for the MLF are:

1. Little or no SO_2, hence the lack of sulphur by those undertaking the *'sur-lies'* method of making Chardonnay; the large majority of these makers have a preference for whole or partial MLF.
2. Relatively low acid levels and a moderate pH, neither of which is easy to come by in cold climates. It is not unusual to see grapes with acid levels of 1.0–1.3 g/l and pH levels around 3.0 when desired levels are acid under 0.9 and pH above 3.4. Many winemakers are more concerned with pH, rather than acid levels, even though they are tied together.
3. Warmer fermentation temperatures. In fact, the marriage of PF and MLF is much happier in barrels where the temperatures find their own level rather than in the controlled temperatures of stainless steel tanks.

Balancing the two fermentations seems to be easily handled by nature, but with much difficulty by man. The MLF can be stopped by several methods, micro-filtration being the most popular.

In all the comparative evaluations I have experienced on three continents, the benefits of MLF, either whole or partial, certainly outweigh any minus factors provided the MLF proceeds smoothly to completion without help from extraneous bacteria. When the MLF has been blamed for ruining a wine, investigation invariably shows that spoilage bacteria interfered with what would have been a normal MLF.

'Sur-lies'

In various forms, yeasts contribute more to the flavour of Chardonnay than to any other wine; more so when the wine is fermented in barrel and aged on its lees, the so-called '*sur-lies*' method. In the *Practical Winery* survey about 35 per cent said they aged on primary lees, indicating that this method has a big following.

After the primary fermentation in barrel is finished, the winemaker has the options of leaving the wine as it is, racking it off its primary lees into new barrels – a fairly common practice – or filtering into clean barrels, a rare happening. Usually winemakers who opt for barrel fermentation go all the way with '*sur-lies*' and this means not adding SO_2 as an anti-oxidant until the MLF is finished. Should the MLF not be desired, a healthy dose of SO_2 will normally inhibit this activity. Before discussing the effects of '*sur-lies*', let us take a glimpse at the barrels themselves, one more eternally debated subject in the New World.

The Choice of Oak Barrels

'From a wine making point of view, the understanding of the wine aroma and flavour effect of oak barrel ageing is as important in some wine styles as the choice of grapes . . .' Winemaker Alan Hoey.

Two thousand years of experience tells us that only the wood of selected white oak trees contribute desirable flavours to wine. Oak containers that lie on their sides are casks, but the term 'barrels' is in common usage and is interchangeable. The most suitable of the ten or more European oaks are the species *Qercus robur* and *Q.sessilis*, while *Q.alba* is the most preferred of seven or eight American varieties.

It is intriguing that slow-growing forests, brought about by climate and soil which provide oak with tighter grain, are more suitable for Chardonnay than the faster growing forests. The closer grained timber appears to provide more in the way of extractables for a longer time than the fast-growing European or American forests.

European white oak forests can be found in Germany, Portugal, Yugoslavia and France. Despite its high cost, French oak is preferred for Chardonnay in France and in the New World. France has a variety of forests located in:

1. **Burgundy** – has small stands of close-grained oak throughout the region. To local winemakers a barrel is a barrel; they do not have the same passion as their New World counterparts about where the oak originated or how the cask was made or toasted. In Burgundy there is but one way to make a barrel. However, by way of clarification, there is an important local body of winemakers known as the Burgundy Oak Research Group who, for the past decade, have been studying all manner of things relating to oak usage. There is a close liaison between this group, the vinegrowers and the coopers. Oak usage studies are also being undertaken in Japan, Australia and Bordeaux.

2. **Centre of France** – covers the popular *départements* of Alliers and Nevers. The forest of Tronçais is within the *département* of Alliers. Because oaks from these forests are tight-grained they have a large following.

3. **Vosge** – a *département* in the northeast of France. On the occasions I have visited Burgundy, there seems to be a widening preference for barrels made from Vosge oak, which has the tightest grain of all.

4. **Limousin** – has been the traditional favourite in the New World. Its open grain appeals to Cognac distillers but is losing popularity among Chardonnay makers around the world due to its relatively short extraction period. Many makers believe that the close-grained northern oaks provide oak flavours over a longer period.

Studies in Japan, where oak flavour is highly important to the distilled spirits (whisky) industry, have identified more than 100 compounds in oak, of which nearly half are aromatic. These compounds are complicated by the various timber drying and splitting methods, and barrel construction practices. Let me explain.

Due mainly to the bourbon industry, the USA is the world's largest user of barrels, and American coopers employ different coopering techniques to their European counterparts. The continental cooper will split the staves (the long, side pieces of a cask) with an axe, while the American way is sawing. Europeans naturally air-dry the wood for periods of up to four years; most American oak for bourbon is kiln-dried although a lot used for wine is air-dried. When shaping the barrel staves the Americans use steam, the French stand the forming barrel over an oak fire and draw the staves together as the wood heats. Now it is this firing that is central to the whole oak flavour argument. The amount the staves are burnt or caramelized will depend on whether it is 'toasted' or 'charred'; there is light, medium and heavy in each category. Each individual category alters the nature of the extractives in the oak, and can dramatically affect the flavour of the wine processed in the cask. And so the elusive search goes on for the 'right' amount of heat. As a general rule in Burgundy, at the most, a light toasting is acceptable. In many cases the cooper is asked to machine this off to bare wood. One of the human factors in this process is that what is medium toast in one cooperage is regarded as heavy toast in another. Accordingly, most wineries tend to stay with one cooper.

The main flavour derivatives from oak are:

1. Oak lactones which give a pronounced 'coconut' smell. There are about twenty times more oak lactones in American oak. These are also major contributors to the perceived 'vanilla' odour.
2. The lignin tannins which are soluble and are an important contributor to wine flavour.
3. Vanillin aldehydes (ethyl vanillin) and other phenolic compounds which enhance odour qualities. These are partially responsible for the smell of vanilla found in red and white wines that have been processed in oak.
4. Compounds formed during the toasting process. Wine-making processes in barrel and moving from barrel to barrel, introduce oxygen into the wine. While this may seem contradictory, some air is desirable for a number of reasons. It is the catalyst for oxidative and maturation processes. Oxygen *per se* is not harmful, it is its management that is difficult. If oxygen is not controlled the winemaker moves from the

wine business to the vinegar trade. Excessive air sets the stage for the acetic acid bacteria irreversibly to destroy the wine. Oxidation also causes browning in Chardonnay, development of bitter flavours, acetaldehyde (sherry character) and loss of fruity aromas.
5. Poly-saccharides – which add to mouth-feel.

Let us return to what is happening in the barrel now that we know what a barrel is all about. The practice of having the wine sit on its lees, which are decomposed yeast cells, is rather new and frightening to many New World winemakers. This process is called yeast autolysis and is an essential part of Champagne's flavour where it is done in each individual bottle. It is the antithesis of much white wine making. But, for Chardonnay, we need the complexity of oak (rather than bubbles) as well as the yeast. Winemaker George Vierra puts it this way, 'The wood tannin and protein yeast lees interact and moderate the wood influence as the autolysis products of the fermentation lees add complexity and depth. The results are wines produced with subtle wood character and full fruit flavours. An unanticipated result of the autolytic activity that we have observed is the continuing freshness of the wines while in contact with the lees.'

Bâtonnage

An essential ingredient of the 'sur-lies' method is regular stirring (bâtonnage) of the yeast lees. Once again, this is a standard Burgundy practice, but a much debated New World subject. 'Regular' can be weekly, fortnightly or monthly, depending on the philosophy of the winemaker. Some makers prefer not to stir the lees at all. My experience suggests that there are no flavour or mouth-feel benefits whatsoever if the lees are not stirred – it would be more beneficial to remove the wine. Bâtonnage nourishes and freshens the wine, in addition to releasing the carbon dioxide that is a by-product of malolactic fermentation, thereby opening the wine to aeration and benefiting the evolutionary processes.

This situation is interesting, in that the presence of the natural CO_2 from the malolactic fermentation keeps oxygen at bay, making the use of SO_2 unnecessary. Winemaker Richard Arrowood says that during this stage of the 'sur-lies' method he has recorded the lowest-ever oxygen levels in his Chardonnays. Should this CO_2 be retained, rather than released by stirring, the wine tends to 'close-in' on itself and possibly end up 'foul'.

The flavour benefits from *bâtonnage* include increased complexity and a 'creamy' texture.

Humidity

Observant visitors to Burgundian wine cellars will have noticed a marked amount of dampness. This is a conscious attempt to maintain a high humidity level, a major aid to maintaining barrels in good condition by retaining moisture in the staves which, in turn, will prevent leaking and, also, lessen evaporation. In the New World, the 'state-of-the-art' winemakers will have air-conditioned and humidity-controlled barrel rooms for fermentation and maturation; these standards have been determined after years of research.

Stainless Steel Tank Fermentation

The alternative to the *'sur-lies'* method, stainless steel fermentation and oak ageing, is possibly the method used to make the 'every-day' drinking wines. After fermentation, usually in minimum 5,000–20,000 litre batches, the wine is normally cleaned by racking, filtering or centrifuging, then pumped into new oak casks for three to nine months for maturation and oak pick-up. In practice, a number of wineries prefer to rack off some of the lees, taking some solids to the new oak. It should be said here that old oak is considered to be a negative winemaking practice. What is *new* and *old* oak? Old oak is considered to be a cask more than four- or five-years-old, which no longer imparts oak flavours to wine.

Following the period in oak the wines will be cold stabilized, then bottled. Cold stabilizing removes tartrates from the wine so that when you buy a bottle of wine it does not have those funny looking crystals floating around in it. This happens naturally throughout Burgundy and many other cold places. In the mechanical method, the wine is placed in a jacketed tank and the temperature is taken down and held below zero for a week or more, precipitating the tartrates.

Once bottled, the Chardonnay is usually held for a bottle-maturation period of six to twelve months before release. The *'sur-lies'* method wines are normally held for a longer period.

In summarizing the two styles, it could be said that the stainless steel fermentations are white, and the *'sur-lies'* method black, and there is an enormous amount of grey in between. The *'sur-lies'* style is definitely meant to be kept and cellared for a minimum of five years from vintage date. The stainless steel styles, with little or no oak, are meant to be 'up-front', fresh, fruity drink-now styles. As the wines have more lees and oak contact they become more complex, requiring a longer evolution period. It is often said that when a stainless steel wine is starting to fall from grace, the *'sur-lies'* wines are just coming into their own.

The Ageing Theory

For some years, there has been an unsubstantiated statistic floating around the wine industry proposing that 80 per cent of all wine purchased is consumed within one week. It does not really matter whether this is 100 per cent correct or not; a gut feeling suggests that it is close to the mark.

Why then is so much time and discussion devoted to how long a wine will age? Who cares anyhow? It is a sad truth that so many wine lovers have never tasted an aged wine, red or white, at its peak of development. Such a wine has all its flavour attributes beautifully integrated – fruit, oak, balance and structure – whereas in its early life the same wine could have been an awkward gangling youth.

Noted California wine scientist, Professor Vernon H. Singleton, has this to say about the ageing process:

> A major role of ageing is to increase the complexity of a wine and this is one reason why ageing alone will not turn an ordinary wine into a great wine. It is possible, for instance, for a wine to contain four different alcohols which, in the course of ageing, could oxidize to four aldehydes which in turn could yield four so-called carboxy acids.
>
> Each of these acids could react, or 'esterify' with a remaining proportion of each of the alcohols, giving a total of sixteen different esters and with the remaining alcohols, aldehydes and

acids – a total of twenty-eight substances arising from the original four.

On the other hand, if oxidation was so severe or prolonged that the four alcohols were completely converted to the four acids, then chemically the wine would be just as complex but would have gained nothing in flavour or quality from the ageing process.

I believe that wines – like people – grow up before they age. Growing up is a process of maturation or evolution; ageing is the development of that character. Not all wines, men or horses benefit from age!

The Mondavi Influence

'Dedicated to Robert Mondavi for his on-going mastery of the Sauvignon Blanc grape' said the label on the 1981 Robert Pecota wine of that variety from Calistoga. Possibly never before had a winemaker paid such a tribute to a fellow winemaker and competitor. A number of organizations, on different occasions, have named Robert Mondavi 'Winemaker of the Year' or something similar and never have I heard a word of dissent.

Yet, strangely, Mondavi is not what one might call a 'qualified' winemaker. Like so many others who have found their niche making wine in California and other parts of the world (training as film-makers, psychologists or anthropologists) Bob Mondavi did not train as a winemaker: he has an economics degree from Stanford University. However, it would be fair to say that few people alive know as much about the craft of winemaking whether it be in France, America or Australia. Born in 1913, he will be at least seventy-five when this book goes to print and he is still imbued with the enthusiasm of a winemaker crushing his first vintage.

In Cyril Ray's book *Robert Mondavi of the Napa Valley*, the author sums up the enigma of the man succinctly when he writes, 'There is a sort of frustrated satisfaction in *not* being satisfied, an excitement in trying every year to beat himself at his own game. This feeling comes through with every interview; every wine.'

The Robert Mondavi Winery (RMW) at Oakville, California, has long been known as the 'test-tube' winery due to experimentation in every facet of winemaking. Comments on these on-going experiments are well covered by Cyril Ray in his comprehensive book on

Mondavi. However, the best known is that done on oak barrels, which caused a world-wide revolution in the use of new oak, particularly 'toasted' and 'charred' barrels. The extension of these experiments has been, and still is, carried out in wineries in almost every country where Chardonnay is made today. And not only Chardonnay. I think it would be fair to say that the University of Bordeaux was sufficiently impressed with the Mondavi approach to oak cask developments, that it followed suit.

In particular, Mondavi pioneered the fermentation of Chardonnay in new oak barrels, something which many people thought was standard Burgundian practice. The truth is that even in the late 1980s, this practice has not been accepted by many leading Burgundians, and at the time Mondavi was leading the way the bulk of Burgundian producers could not afford to indulge in this expensive technique. Regardless, this method has produced some of the greatest Chardonnays of the decade and, in the minds of many, has put the Mondavi Chardonnay among the world's best wines.

Robert Mondavi is the ultimate student jetsetter. For a quarter of a century he has made at least one pilgrimage annually to France, to study and observe what and how Bordelais and Burgundian winemakers and viticulturists are doing. There is no doubt at all in my mind, that Robert Mondavi was not the only one learning in these exchanges.

In addition to Italy, his parental homeland, the 'Napa Nomad' also seems to make an annual visit 'down-under' – both he and his wife, Margrit, have an abiding affection for both Australia and New Zealand. Robert was involved in the initial development of Western Australia's now famous Leeuwin (pronounced Loo-in) Estate winery in the Margaret River area. It is interesting to see the Mondavi 'stamp' of philosophy in so much at Leeuwin, from the winery equipment to the summer concerts on the lawns. Even if these two wineries are on opposite sides of the globe (the very reason for the termination of the RMW involvement in Western Australia), the same Mondavi gospel works almost next door in the Napa Valley at Mike Grgich's, or in the adjoining Sonoma Valley at Simi where the articulate Zelma Long shapes artistic Chardonnays year after year. Both are former technicians at RMW.

Many California wine folk will tell you that RMW is all about Cabernet (in fact although his great wines are labelled Cabernet Sauvignon, they always contain some Cabernet Franc and, on occasions, Merlot). The ultimate wine scoop was when RMW combined with Baron Philippe de Rothschild of Mouton-

Rothschild to make the much-discussed Opus One. Not only did this signify the peak of international acceptance, it also signified that two great men from two cultural extremes were prepared to unite for their mutual interest, and for the world of better wine; something so many lesser people within a single culture are incapable of doing. In spite of all this, the Robert Mondavi winery has been the home of California Chardonnay technology. A few others may, possibly, have done it better; nobody, anywhere, has done it on such a large scale.

The RMW could justifiably be called 'the million case boutique'. As UK wine importer Geoffrey Roberts says, 'I can think of no other winery in the world which produces wines of such exceptional quality in such enormous quantity . . . Those million and a half or so cases a year are more important than the 2,000 cases a year from a typical "boutique" winery; not because there are 700 times as many bottles, but because of the quality of the wine they contain – and the quality of the man who makes them . . .'

If you think Bob Mondavi is at the pinnacle of wine knowledge or success, you would be wrong. 'We're just at the beginning; it's so exciting!' said Robert Mondavi when interviewed at the completion of the 1987 California vintage. 'If you think our 1985 Chardonnay is good, just wait until you taste our 1986, which is better, and the 1987, which is the best wine we've ever made. California Chardonnays will be constantly changing for years to come. Wine-making starts in the vineyard, where we are doing experimental work with our vines, beginning to get better selection of land by eliminating those that are not quite as good, and changing our methods of viticultural practice. In the winery, too, we are carrying on an enormous amount of research work with

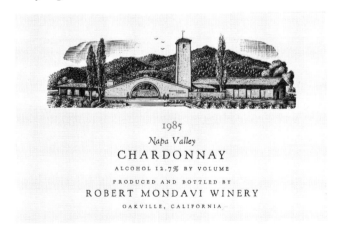

1985
Napa Valley
CHARDONNAY
ALCOHOL 12.7% BY VOLUME
PRODUCED AND BOTTLED BY
ROBERT MONDAVI WINERY
OAKVILLE, CALIFORNIA

Chardonnay. For instance, *bâtonnage* changes the style of wine completely. We stirred the lees a certain way and it took us away from the oakiness, to give a leaner, livelier wine. Really we are just getting started. This thing is exciting.

'At Woodbridge, we don't crush the grapes anymore, we take the whole bunch and press them Champagne style and we are going to do that here (Oakville) this coming year too. This year we have put in three huge presses at Woodbridge and it really makes a difference.'

At the RMW, the search for better and best is relentless. Some of his on-going experiments will be adopted everywhere, some in a few places, some in none at all. But one thing is for sure: the 'Mondavi Influence', whether acknowledged or not, will continue to be felt wherever wine is made.

AFTERWORD

L ondon-based *Decanter* magazine, regarded by many as the world's most authoritative wine journal, conducted an international Chardonnay tasting of eighty-two wines in mid-1988. The judges were a blend of importers (from Burgundy, California, South Africa and Australasia) with specialized knowledge and Masters of Wine. The event was regarded as one of the most representative ever conducted, in view of the wide range of commercial wines, and this tasting was significant in that we were able to measure the enormous progress that has been made from a standing start only a few years ago.

There were about ten or more wines from Australia, Burgundy and Chablis combined, California, Italy, New Zealand, and South Africa. There were also isolated wines from Bulgaria, Portugal, Canada, Spain and the Loire, and even one from Idaho, USA.

Once again, three of the wines (two Australian and one California) that have consistently been chosen in the top four in previous panel tastings for this book were clear favourites, with the Napa Valley 1985 Robert Mondavi wine outstanding.

The significance of the *Decanter* tasting can best be summed up by one of the judges who commented: 'The French are cleaning up their act and the styles of the New World and Burgundy are coming closer together. Only a couple of years ago it was easy to smell a glass and identify its origin. Nowadays, this is very difficult with the top wines.'

Yet another comparative tasting of Chardonnay from Burgundy and California was held by the Munich/Zurich-based wine magazine, *Vinum*, during 1987.

Once again, their tasters selected a California wine (Cuvaison) as the best, and overall the California wines smothered the Burgundy wines (in this instance a very distinguished lot from the excellent

1985 vintage). Let me return to the early pages of this book and my conclusions about international judgements; I don't think they matter. But (and a rather substantial but) if panels like the two above continue to select wines from the New World and declare them as good as, if not better than, the original product, one must conclude that a lot of people are judging the quality of the wine in the bottle, rather than being impressed by the name on the label.

Chardonnay experimentation knows no bounds – from Austria to Zimbabwe – and as yet, it is early days in most countries including Italy, Spain, Bulgaria, Canada and South Africa.

However, it does appear that scientists, growers, makers, merchants and educators all over the world are caressing and tutoring the thoroughbred that is Chardonnay. Every day, in every country, I see all sorts of people just pushing that little bit further in the hope of extending our knowledge, and the flavour of this wonderful wine.

Now, dear reader, it is up to you to monitor how successful these efforts have been, today, next year and in the years ahead.

Personally, I just can't wait for the future!

Alan Young
London 1988

GLOSSARY

Acidity Tartness, the sharp taste of natural grape acid. Contributes to the flavour and keeping qualities of the wine. Not to be confused with 'sourness'.

After Taste The 'shadow' of the wine after swallowing. Can reveal an extra attribute or fault.

Ampelography Study of grape varieties.

Appellation Contrôlée (AC/AOC) French wine laws that dictate almost everything to do with grapegrowing and winemaking. Not a guarantee of quality.

Aroma Fragrance of wine coming from the grape.

Balance An evaluative term – a wine in which the acid, sugar, bitterness, alcohol and flavour are in harmony.

Barrique An oak barrel of 225 litres.

Baumé Used in Australia as a measure of sugar in grape juice or wine. One degree of *Baumé* equals 1.8 per cent of sugar. *Brix* is another measure of sugar.

Big A tasting term. Wine of extra viscosity, flavour or alcohol.

Biscuit A flavour term associated with Chardonnay and Champagne.

Bitter A tasting term; registers at the back of the mouth.

Blanc de Blancs A Champagne term. White wine made from white (Chardonnay) grapes.

Blanc de Noir Another Champagne term, adopted by other winemakers to denote white wine made from red/black grapes (Pinot Noir).

Body Viscosity, consistency, thickness or texture. Reflects the amount of alcohol and sugar.

Bouquet The part of the *nose* (q.v.) which originates from fermentation and ageing processes – with *aroma* (q.v.) makes up the total nose.

Brix (Bricks or Balling) A hydrometer calibrated measure of sugar – used in Europe and USA.

Brut The drier type of champagne.

Character Smell and taste term – referring to vinosity and style.

Clarity Clearness – opposite to turbid.

Clean Wine free of off-flavours or tastes.

Clone A sub-variety or strain that has developed within a particular grape variety.

Cloying Excessive sugar in sweet white wines.

Condition Clarity and soundness.

Coarse Open texture, normally faulty, often oxidized.

Crémant A style of Champagne from the Côtes de Blancs denoting less pressure, also made in Alsace, Burgundy and Loire.

Crisp Usually refers to white wines of good acidity that stimulate the taste senses. A characteristic of grapes grown in cool climates.

Dry Opposite to sweet – without sugar.

Dumb A tasting term signifying lack of development/character.

Earthy Indicating the wine has a taste or smell of the soil.

Estate Bottled Bottled at the winery adjoining the vineyards where the grapes were grown. Local interpretations have broadened this original meaning.

Ethyl Alcohol The purest alcohol – not poisonous to the human system. A product of ferment grape juice.

Extraction Extraction is what makes red wine different to white wine. Extraction during fermentation produces the colour pigments, tannins and aromatic substances.

Fermentation The miracle of turning grape juice to wine. Yeast enzymes convert grape sugars to ethyl alcohol and carbon dioxide.

Fining Clarifying wine before bottling using egg whites or colloidal clay, which sink to the bottom carrying with them minute substances that were held in suspension.

Finish Last impression left in the mouth by the smell and taste.

Flabby Too much fruit, too little acid and usually coarse.

Flavour Flavour is a combination of odour, taste, temperature and texture.

Flowery Pleasantly aromatic – in young white wines with freshness.

Fruity Aroma and flavour of fresh grapes.

Generic Wine names which refer to historical or geographical areas, e.g. Burgundy, Moselle, Sherry, Port.

Green Common to taste and smell; excessive fruit acid-sharp flavour.

Hard Dry, almost bitter, unpleasant, too much acid.

Hot A wine with too much alcohol and not enough fruit to balance.

Light A confusing term that can apply to the alcoholic strength of a wine. A full-bodied wine can be light on flavour.

Méthode Champenoise The bottle fermentation/traditional method of making champagne which includes disgorging by hand.

Must Crushed grapes or juice until the end of fermentation.

Neutral Lacking in flavour.

Nose The combined bouquet and aroma of wine.

Oaky Flavour obtained by ageing wine in new oak casks.

Oenology The science of wine and winemaking.

Oxidation Change in wine caused by exposure to air. Can have beneficial effects, but over-exposure brings about discoloration and loss of flavour.

Oxidation–Reduction Reactions Oxidation and reduction always occur simultaneously with the transfer of electrons. The substances that gain and lose electrons are referred to respectively as the oxidizing and reducing agents.

Phenolics   Phenolics are basically the colour pigments (antho-cyanins) and tannins which provide astringency.

Pungent   Strong, aromatic, often earthy smell.

Racking   Moving wine from a cask in which it has deposited sediment to a clean container.

Residual Sugar   Normally in a white wine where fermentation has been arrested to allow some natural grape sugar to remain.

Retro-Olfactory   Or retro-nasal. Smelling through the mouth.

Round   A wine harmoniously balanced, in body and flavour.

Savour   The 'smell' when exhaling through the mouth.

Soft   A wine low in astringency or alcohol.

Sour   Disagreeably acid, acetic acid – vinegary.

Spicy   Wines of pronounced varietal character – Muscat and Gewürztraminer are good examples.

Supple   Mouth filling, easy to drink.

Tannin   A complex natural substance in wine obtained from the skins, seeds and oak casks. More evident in red wines for which it is essential if the wine is to improve with age.

Tart   Possessing agreeable acidity from the natural fruit acid.

Thin   Lack of body, watery.

Varietal   Wine name taken from the grape variety.

Viticulture   The study and practice of grape production.

Vignoble   Winegrowing area.

Vigneron   Winemaker.

Vintage   Harvesting of grapes and converting grapes to wine.

Vintner   Wine-merchant.

Vinosity   A tasting term relating to grape character and alcoholic strength of wine.

Volatile   Evaporating easily in the form of a vapour – gaseous or in the gas phase.

Volatile Acids   Acids that are steam distillable – acetic, butyric, formic and propionic.

BIBLIOGRAPHY

Absolutely essential reading:

George, Rosemary. *The Wines of Chablis* (Sotheby, 1984)
Hanson, Anthony. *Burgundy* (Faber and Faber, 1982)
Sutcliffe, Serena. *Pocket Guide to the Wines of Burgundy* (Mitchell Beazley, 1986)

Recommended reading:

Arlott, John and Fielden, Christopher. *Burgundy: Vines and Wines* (Quartet, 1978)
Delaforce, Patrick. *Burgundy on a Budget* (Mildmay, 1987)
Jackson, D. and Schuster, D. *The Production of Grapes and Wine in Cool Climates* (Butterworth, 1987)
Johnson, Hugh and Duijker, Hubrecht. *The Wine Atlas of France and Travellers Guide* (Mitchell Beazley, 1987)
The Macdonald Guide to French Wines, First Edition (1986)
New Zealand Society of Oenology and Viticulture. *Proceedings: Second International Cool Climate Symposium 1988*
Robinson, Jancis. *Vines, Grapes and Wines* (Mitchell Beazley, 1986)
Young, Alan. *An Encounter with Wine* (International Wine Academy, 1986)
Young, Alan. *Making Sense of Wine Tasting* (Lennard, 1987)
Yoxall, H. W. *The Wines of Burgundy* (Penguin, 1974)

INDEX

Page numbers in *italic* refer to the illustrations